Unlocking the Secrets of Research

Anita Meyer Meinbach, Ed.D.
Liz Christman Rothlein, Ed.D.

University of Miami
Coral Gables, Florida

Scott, Foresman and Company
Glenview, Illinois   London

 **Good Year Books**

are available for preschool through grade 12 and for every basic curriculum subject plus many enrichment areas. For more Good Year Books, contact your local bookseller or educational dealer. For a complete catalog with information about other Good Year Books, please write:

Good Year Books
Department GYB
1900 East Lake Avenue
Glenview, Illinois 60025

Contents

Introduction

Today, more than ever before in our history, there is a voluminous amount of information available. Teachers can not expect students to remember all the information that has been compiled; however, it is important for them to learn where to look for specific types of information.

Traditionally, students have consulted general encyclopedias for information they need. However, there are many other sources which can be used to locate information, such as thesauruses, atlases, almanacs, books of facts, and so forth. The general encyclopedia may not provide all the information that is necessary; therefore, this workbook has been designed to introduce students to a variety of reference books and to give them practical application in using these books.

Rationale

Uncovering information can be an adventure in itself. Once students are familiar with a variety of reference books, they can use their skills of analysis to choose the appropriate books that best meet their needs. A natural outcome of exposing students to the material in a variety of reference books is in the improved quality of the information they receive. Actively involving students in the search for information will make learning much more meaningful.

Objectives

Unlocking the Secrets of Research is designed to enable the students to fulfill several objectives. By using the Study Guides, Activity Sheets, and other activities in this book the student will:

- develop research skills
- become familar with a variety of reference books
- become skilled in using the selected reference books
- learn to focus research topics and choose appropriate reference books
- develop skills in using footnotes, indexes, appendices, and graphic information
- develop the higher order thinking skills of analysis, synthesis, and evaluation
- become knowledgeable on a given topic
- write a bibliography
- develop independent working skills
- be stimulated and motivated to pursue further research interests

Features

Throughout *Unlocking the Secrets of Research*, questions have been developed which not only foster students' research skills, but also encourage students to use the higher order thinking skills of analysis, synthesis, and evaluation. A variety of worksheets are included to meet the book's objectives.

Study Guides

In chapters one through four reproducible ''Study Guides'' are provided to introduce the students to each of the references selected. One of the purposes of the Study Guide is to acquaint students with the variety of information that can be found in

each assigned reference book. A second purpose of the Study Guide is to help students discover how to locate and utilize the information available in each of the reference books.

Following a brief introduction to each of the reference books by the teacher or librarian, the teacher can assign individuals or small groups to a reference book by providing the appropriate Study Guide for that particular book. The students should be given ample time to peruse the assigned reference book and complete the Study Guide. Students can work individually or in small groups. An answer key is provided at the back of this book. Study Guides can be self-correcting or checked by the teacher.

The Study Guide can also be used by the teacher as a diagnostic tool or pretest. Following the completion of each Study Guide, the teacher can teach any additional skills necessary for using the reference books.

Activity Sheets

In the first three chapters, reproducible "Activity Sheets" are provided for each selected reference book and/or topic presented in *Unlocking the Secrets of Research*. The major purpose of the Activity Sheets is to provide students with the opportunity to become more proficient in the use of reference books. A natural outcome of the Activity Sheets is that the students will gain valuable information on a variety of subjects they will be researching. The Activity Sheets should be assigned to the students *after* they have successfully completed the Study Guide for a particular reference book.

Often the Activity Sheets are designated "Activity Sheet A" or "Activity Sheet B." Activity Sheet A questions are generally less complex than those on Activity Sheet B. Teachers may assign less capable researchers to Activity Sheets A and the more sophisticated researchers to Activity Sheets B or each student may be assigned Activity Sheet A to complete first and then go into more depth by completing Activity Sheet B.

An answer key is provided at the back of this book. The Activity Sheets can be self-checking or teacher checked. However, many of the questions require open-ended answers which would need to be read by someone other than the writer.

In Chapters IV and V, the Activity Sheets have been designed to aid the students in utilizing the skills developed in the first three chapters. These Activity Sheets will help the students to understand the function of bibliographies, footnotes, and endnotes. The Activity Sheets will also aid students in learning how to focus on a topic, select the appropriate reference books, organize their material, and then outline their research papers.

Both the Activity Sheets and Study Guides used in this book are based on the reference books listed below. It is realized there are other reference books that contain similar information; therefore, if you are unable to obtain the reference books listed, you may substitute with other appropriate materials.

- Bartlett's Book of Familiar Quotations
- Current Biography Yearbook
- Dictionary
- Encyclopedia
- Encyclopedia of Careers and Vocational Guidance

- Famous First Facts
- Guinness Book of World Records
- Readers' Guide to Periodical Literature
- Thesaurus
- Twentieth Century Authors
- Webster's Biographical Dictionary
- Who's Who in America
- World Almanac
- World Atlas

What Did You Uncover? Sheets

A reproducible "What Did You Uncover?" section is included for each reference book and is intended to be completed *after* the student has done both the Study Guide and the Activity Sheet(s) assigned. The purpose of What Did You Uncover? is to encourage the students to evaluate the reference material they have just used.

Review Sheets

A reproducible "Review Sheet" is provided at the end of Chapters I, II, and III. The Review Sheets are intended to review skills and information gained as a result of completing the Study Guide, Activity Sheets, and What Did You Uncover? sections. An answer key for the Review Sheets is provided at the back of this book.

Organization

Unlocking the Secrets of Research is divided into five chapters.

Chapter I — Selected Reference Books
Chapter II — Readers' Guide to Periodical Literature
Chapter III — Encyclopedias
Chapter IV — Writing a Bibliography, Footnotes, and Endnotes
Chapter V — Applying Your Research Skills

Chapter I contains a Study Guide section and a What Did You Uncover? section to help students better understand the purpose of each assigned reference book, plus twenty-four Activity Sheets for use with each of the twelve reference books (two Activity Sheets per reference book), and a Review Sheet.

Chapter II includes a Study Guide to help students understand the purpose of using the *Readers' Guide to Periodical Literature*. Activity Sheets to develop and enhance the students' ability to use this reference book effectively, and a Review Sheet.

Chapter III provides a Study Guide to introduce students to the diverse types of material found in encyclopedias. If more than one type of encyclopedia is available, ask students to complete a study guide for each type (i.e., Science Encyclopedia, General Encyclopedia, Music Encyclopedia). This chapter contains Activity Sheets which have been divided into different interest areas to motivate the students to pursue a variety of topics and subject areas. A Review Sheet is also included in this chapter.

Chapters IV and V are designed to develop skills in utilizing information gained in the first three chapters. Chapter IV contains Study Guides and Activity Sheets for writing a bibliography and footnotes/endnotes. It is suggested that teachers obtain a copy of *A Manual for Writers of Term Papers, Theses, and Dissertations,* 4th edition, by Kate L. Turabian, University of Chicago Press, and make it available to students involved in research. Chapter V contains Activity Sheets to develop skills in writing a research paper.

Upon successful completion of the *Unlocking the Secrets of Research* worksheets, students will be able to enjoy and understand the basic essentials for using reference books to pursue a given topic.

How to Use This Book

The following steps should be taken to assure maximum success for students using these materials:

1. Discuss what is meant by the term ''reference book.''

2. Take students to the school library and point out the location of reference books listed in the Annotated Bibliography.

   NOTE: Make available as many reference books as possible in the classroom. If they are not available in the school library, seek other sources. Many of the reference books are available in paperback form and are relatively inexpensive.

3. Give students a brief overview of each reference book (use the Annotated Bibliography at the back of this book as a guide).

4. Encourage students to investigate reference books in other locations — home, local libraries, etc. Ask students to share these books with you and members of the class.

5. Discuss procedures for completing materials for each reference book (i.e., first complete the Study Guide, second complete the Activity Sheet(s) assigned, third complete the What Did You Uncover? section, and finally complete the review sheets.

6. Assign a variety of reference books so that everyone doesn't need to use the same reference book at the same time.

   NOTE: Individual pages can be reproduced and assigned on a daily basis or students can be given a complete set of materials for one reference book and be instructed to work through it independently.

While students are involved independently on reproducible pages, the teacher may wish to work with individuals or small groups in furthering development of research skills, (i.e., using footnotes, indexes, and so forth). In addition, these materials may be developed into a unit on research or each reference book may be developed into a learning center.

Additional Activities

The following activities have been designed to allow the classroom teacher to extend the skills developed in *Unlocking the Secrets of Research*.

Bartlett's Book of Familiar Quotations

1. Solicit a favorite quotation from each student and ask which famous person said it. Ask students to illustrate their quotation. Compile these quotations into a "Favorite Quotations" booklet for each member of the class.

2. Ask students to choose a person whose quotations are included in *Familiar Quotations*. Have them select their favorite quotations and illustrate each (i.e., Shakespeare's best).

Current Biography Yearbook

1. Group students into pairs. Tell them to inteview each other and then write each other's biography. Compile biographies into a "Current Biographies of _____ Class" booklet.

2. Using magazine articles, books, etc., ask students to write a biography similar to one found in the *Current Biography Yearbook*. It should be about a famous living person who is not listed in the yearbook.

Dictionary

1. Ask the students to find out who is credited with writing the first dictionary. Give them the opportunity to research this famous person and write a report to include interesting facts about the development and developer of the dictionary. They can present their findings in a creative manner.

2. Encourage the students to listen to the evening news for a specified period of time and keep a diary of words they hear on the news but don't understand. Have them make up several activity sheets which they and other classmates can use to learn the meanings of the words in the diary (i.e., crossword puzzles). The teacher can duplicate each person's word list and activity sheets and put together a class "Vocabulary Book."

3. Ask the students to find twenty-six words to describe themselves. Each word should begin with a different letter of the alphabet. Encourage them to choose uncommon words.

4. Divide the class into groups of four or five. Give each group a dictionary. The group leader then calls out a word. The first group to go to the chalkboard and write the guide words for the page where the word was found gets a point.

Encyclopedia of Careers and Vocational Guidance

1. Invite people who represent a variety of careers to come into the classroom and speak to the group about their careers. Have students prepare questions they want to ask these people.

2. Ask students to write to selected businesses in a field which they are interested. Tell them to ask for information regarding a specific job — salary, qualifications, training, and any other additional criteria the business might look for in a potential employee.

3. Plan field trips in which students have the opportunity to observe a variety of careers firsthand. Also plan trips to a local vocational school.

Famous First Facts

1. Have the class create their own *Famous First Facts* book using incidents relating to their state, city, and school.

2. Have students skim through *Famous First Facts* and find three facts especially interesting to them. Have them do additional research on these subjects.

3. Have students create an advertisement to familiarize people with *Famous First Facts*.

Guinness Book of World Records

1. Plan with the students to have a record-breaking contest for their own class or school. Set up relays, contests, and athletic events. Ask students to record each event's winner and compile data. This could continue each year to see if school and/or class records could be broken.

2. Ask the entire class (or just interested individuals) to write to the Guinness publishers and find out how to challenge a world record. Encourage students to attempt any feat they believe they can do which would enable them to break a record and

result in getting their names in the *Guinness Book of World Records*. As a safety precaution, students should have their idea(s) approved by the teacher before they attempt to break any record.

Thesaurus

1. Have students rewrite a creative writing paper using the thesaurus to find words which would make the paper more interesting while not changing the meaning.

2. Ask students to choose an artist from a list of suggested ones and look through art books to select a painting done by this artist. Have them describe the picture, using the thesaurus to paint the picture with words.

3. Brainstorm with the class. What words do they use too often? Make a list of synonyms they could substitute for each word.

Twentieth Century Authors

1. Have students select a partner. With this partner they will write an entry for a favorite writer to appear in *Twentieth Century Authors*. They may try to get information about the author through the publisher or directly from the writer if he/she is still living.

2. Have an "author fair" (similar to a book fair). The students can dress up as their favorite author and talk about themselves.

3. Play a "To Tell the Truth" game in which three people claim to be a famous author. Of the three, only one has read *Twentieth Century Authors* and knows the important facts relating to this person.

4. Tell students to choose an author whose work they enjoy. Encourage them to write this person and ask how he/she became a writer and what advice he/she can offer to budding authors.

Webster's Biographical Dictionary

1. Ask students to read a biography on the life of a famous person who is not included in *Webster's Biographical Dictionary* and complete an entry on this person following the format of this reference book.

2. Have students compare and contrast *Webster's Biographical Dictionary* with two other biographical dictionaries.

3. Ask students to prepare a commercial or an advertisement to persuade others to use *Webster's Biographical Dictionary*.

Who's Who in America

1. Ask students to each think of someone they like and respect in the school or neighborhood. They can write a biography similar to those found in *Who's Who in America* and compile a "Who's Who in _____." (Insert the name of your town, city, or school.)

2. Ask each student to select someone from the current *Who's Who in America* who, in their opinion, appeared to be very special. Have students get into small groups and defend their selections. Ask them to reach a consensus on one of the people selected who they feel is the most worthy of being listed in this publication.

World Almanac

1. Ask the class to create tables and charts relating to their own communities. They should include information such as daily weather, historic sites, public schools, private schools, and so forth. This could be a project that could continue throughout the year.

2. Ask students to look through the almanac and find information about the economical status of their state as compared to other states. They could investigate the salaries of governors and teachers, income from national resources, etc. and prepare a chart or graph to illustrate their findings.

World Atlas

1. Ask each student to choose a city and/or country they would like to visit. After they have made their selection, direct them to compile an informational packet. They will include information on population, climate, annual rainfall, major vegetation, terrain, etc. In addition to this information, suggest they write to Chamber of Commerces, tourist agencies, embassies, and other appropriate agencies to get additional information.

2. Ask students to make a poster advertising a favorite place to visit.

Encyclopedias

Where in the World Am I?

1. As a class project, have students develop questions for a "trivia" game which deals with unusual, interesting places. You can limit questions to whichever countries-/continents you wish to include.

2. Have the class create a "patchwork map" from scraps of material. Label interesting places and points of interest.

3. Turn your class into a travel agency! Each small group can become "specialists" on a certain geographic area. Have them prepare their own travel brochures, complete with illustrations and text, to lure others to visit the area.

4. Have students prepare a route which will take them around the world. Ask them to trace this route on a map and then determine the distance traveled, methods of transportation, and time trip would take.

Piñatas, Fireworks, and Totem Poles

1. Ask students to share "special customs" which they feel are unique to their families.

2. Have each student choose their favorite holiday and tell about the custom they like best regarding that holiday.

3. As a class project, make a piñata or totem pole.

What Makes It Tick?

1. Ask the students to choose an invention they are particularly interested in and make a diagram to illustrate how it operates. These could also be developed for a sharing session with classmates.

2. Encourage students to collect discarded or unwanted mechanical items from home, neighbors, and relatives. Provide the students with the opportunity to investigate these items by taking them apart and, if possible, putting them back together.

Somewhere Over the Rainbow

1. Encourage students to create a time-line on developments in the space program.

2. Have students write a letter to their favorite astronaut. Suggest they include several questions they'd like the astronaut to address.

3. Let students create a science fiction story (based on some facts) about a ``Journey into the Bermuda Triangle'' or a ``Journey into the Black Hole.''

4. Encourage students to write to NASA to request up-to-date information on its recent findings and projects planned.

5. Ask students to prepare a chart to illustrate how orbiting satellites work.

All Animals Great and Small

1. Ask students to select an animal (other than a cat, dog, or bird) which they would like to have as a pet. They can research this animal to find out as much as possible about it. Information should be included about the country in which it originated, what kinds of food it eats, type of habitat, size when fully grown, etc.

2. Tell students to peruse the encyclopedia to find information on animals. They should choose three unusual animals and write a brief description of each on note cards. They can distribute the cards to friends who will guess the names of the animals.

Chapter I

Selected Reference Books

Bartlett's Book of Familiar Quotations

Study Guide

Directions: Using Bartlett's *Familiar Quotations,* complete the following:

1. Name of reference book _____

2. Fill in the following information:

   Author _____

   Publisher _____

   Place of Publication_____

   Date of Publication _____

3. In the beginning of the book you will find a "Guide to the Use of *Familiar Quotations.*" Briefly read this guide. In your own words, explain what "lb" means.

   _____

4. What type of information is found in this reference book?

   _____

   _____

5. How do you find the information you need? (i.e. alphabetically, by subject, author, etc.?) _____

   _____

6. When looking up a subject in the index, you will notice a page number followed by a colon and a second number (i.e. 700:4). The 700 refers to the page number. What do you think the number 4 means?_____

   _____

What Did You Uncover?

Directions: Upon completion of the assigned activity sheet(s), answer the following:

1. What is unique or special about Bartlett's *Familiar Quotations*?

   _____

2. When might it be necessary to consult *Familiar Quotations*?

   _____

3. What did you find most interesting about this reference book?

   _____

Name _____ Date _____

Bartlett's Book of Familiar Quotations

Activity Sheet A

Directions: Using the Bartlett's Book of *Familiar Quotations*, answer the following:

1. What advice did Confucius give on the subject of learning? _____
   _____

2. Choose one quotation on the topic of "dreams." Write the quotation and its
   author. _____
   _____
   _____

3. What did John F. Kennedy say at his inaugural address on January 20, 1961,
   about what you can do for your country?
   _____
   _____

4. What did John Lennon and Paul McCartney ask about lonely people?
   _____
   What song is this from? _____

5. Woody Allen has a quote which is also the title of a film. What is it?
   _____
   In what year was it written? _____

6. Who wrote the quote, "No one can make you feel inferior without your consent"?
   _____
   Do you agree with this quote? _____ Why or why not?
   _____
   _____

7. Who did Muhammad Ali believe to be the greatest person in the world?
   _____
   By what name was Muhammad Ali formerly known?
   _____

8. In what book by Mary Shelley was "the wretch—the miserable monster" created?
   _____

Bartlett's Book of Familiar Quotations

Activity Sheet B

Directions: Using the Bartlett's Book of *Familiar Quotations*, answer the following:

1. Who is credited with writing the following quotation, "Eat to live, and not live to eat"? _____

   _____

   For what publication did he write this quotation? _____

   _____

2. What did Lewis Carroll, the author of *Alice's Adventures in Wonderland*, say would happen if everyone minded their own business? (Hint: the Duchess said it.)

   _____

3. Choose a quotation by Martin Luther King, Jr. that you especially like. Copy the quotation and tell what it means to you. _____

   _____

   _____

   _____

4. "So foul and fair a day I have not seen," is a famous quotation by William Shakespeare. What play is it from? _____

   Have you ever known a day to be foul and fair at the same time?_____

   What could this mean? _____

   _____

   _____

5. Fill in the blanks of this famous quote by Isaac Bashevis Singer: "What nature delivers to us is never _____. Because what nature creates has _____ in it." Explain what this quotation means.

   _____

   _____

6. In Aesop's fable, "Hercules and the Wagoner," what is said about the gods?

   _____

   After the quote you will see a small number. This refers you to a footnote at the bottom of the page. This footnote shows you other versions of this quotation. Read them and then write your own version.

   _____

Name _____ 🔑 Date _____

Current Biography Yearbook

Study Guide

Directions: Using the *Current Biography Yearbook,* complete the following:

1. Name of reference book _____

2. Fill in the following information:

   Author/Editor _____

   Publisher _____

   Place of Publication_____

   Date of Publication _____

3. What is the purpose of the *Current Biography Yearbook?*

   _____

   _____

4. How often is the *Current Biography Yearbook* published?_____

5. How do you find someone's biography in this reference book? _____

   _____

   How do you know which *Current Biography Yearbook* to look into to find a biography on a person who has done something significant between the years 1940-1970?

   _____

   How would you find a biography for a person who has done something significant between 1971-1980?

   _____

   _____

6. At the end of each biography there are references. What is the purpose of this?

   _____

   _____

   In the references, what does ''pors'' mean?

   _____

7. References for periodicals and newspapers are abbreviated. How can you find out what these abbreviations mean?

   _____

8. What appears in the heading of each biography?

   _____

▼

Current Biography Yearbook

Study Guide Continued

9. In the index, what is meant by the date following the name? _____
    _____

    What does it mean if you find "obit" following a name in the index?
    _____

    For whom are "obits" published?_____
    _____

10. How can you tell if an article has been written about a person in an earlier publication
    of the *Current Biography Yearbook?*
    _____
    _____

What Did You Uncover?

Directions: Upon completion of the activity sheet(s) assigned, answer the following:

1. Write the name of someone that you felt should have a biography in the *Current
    Biography Yearbook* that didn't.
    _____

    Why do you think he/she should be included in this book?_____
    _____
    _____

2. What was most helpful to you in the *Current Biography Yearbook* in regard to
    locating the information you wanted? _____
    _____
    _____

3. When might it be necessary for you to consult the *Current Biography Yearbook?*
    _____
    _____
    _____

Current Biography Yearbook

Activity Sheet A

Directions: Using the *Current Biography Yearbook*, complete the following:

1. What has made Evel Knievel famous? _____

   _____

   What does he like to be called? _____

   In what high school activities was he involved? _____

   _____

   For several years, Evel Knievel was a car thief, con man, and safecracker. To whom does he contribute much of his own success and recuperation?

   _____

   _____

2. If you wanted to read biographies on people who were famous in 1983 for some sports accomplishment, how would you find their names?

   _____

   _____

   Choose one of the people in sports whose biography is listed in the 1983 *Current Biography Yearbook,* Read the biography and then provide the following information: What is his/her occupation?

   _____

   What do you think was this person's greatest accomplishment?_____

   _____

   In what country does this person live? _____

   What was the most interesting thing that you found out about this person?

   _____

3. In your opinion, what makes Eddie Murphy famous?_____

   _____

   How old is he?_____ What is considered his first step toward superstardom?

   _____

   Who is Eddie Murphy's comedy idol?_____

   Do you agree with his choice? _____ Why or why not? _____

   _____

Current Biography Yearbook

Activity Sheet A Continued

After reading the biography, what do you like best about this person?

_____

4. For what is Ronald Reagan best known? _____

    How old is Mr. Reagan? _____ Where was Mr. Reagan born? _____

    What other occupations has Mr. Reagan had? _____

    _____

    What is Mr. Reagan's ancestory? _____

    After reading Mr. Reagan's biography, what two things do you feel influenced him the most in achieving success?_____

    _____

5. Bill Rodgers, a popular marathon runner, succeeded what other great runner as the American "king of the road"? _____

    What other occupation does Bill Rodgers have in addition to running?

    _____

    At the time his biography was written, how many marathon titles had he won? _____ What person, during his college years, had a major influence on Mr. Rodgers in regard to his running?_____

    _____

    Of all the feats achieved and records broken by Bill Rodgers, which do you feel is the most important?_____

    Why?_____

6. In the space provided, write your own biography, as you'd like to see it appear in the *Current Biography Yearbook.* _____

    _____

    _____

    _____

    _____

    _____

    _____

Name _____ 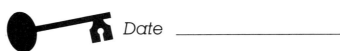 Date _____

Current Biography Yearbook

Activity Sheet B

Directions: Using the *Current Biography Yearbook,* complete the following:

1. After reading the biographies of Jennifer Holliday and Beverly Sills, what similarities do you find between these two people?

   _____

   _____

   What differences do you find? _____

   _____

   What do you think is Beverly Sill's greatest accomplishment? _____

   _____

   Why? _____

   _____

   For what is Jennifer Holliday best known? _____

   Which person would you most like to meet? _____

   Why? _____

   _____

2. For what is Grace Kelly best known? _____

   For what film did she win an Oscar? _____

   To whom was she married? _____

   How did her romance with him begin? _____

   _____

   How many children did they have?_____ What caused Grace Kelly's death?

   _____

   When did she die? _____

3. What do Sally Ride and Valentina Tereshkova have in common?

   _____

   _____

   How many years apart did this accomplishment occur?_____ What hobby
   does Valentina Tereshkova have? _____

   What hobbies does Sally Ride have? _____

▼

Current Biography Yearbook

Activity Sheet B Continued

What similarities and/or differences do you see in the training or preparation of these two women in regard to their accomplishments?

_____

_____

4. List two *Current Biography Yearbooks* which have a biography written about George Bush? _____ and _____

   Why do you think he had a biography written in two different yearbooks?

   _____

   What does the name (Herbert Walker) appearing in brackets after his name, mean? _____

   _____

   After reading his biography, what do you think is his most important contribution to the United States? _____

   _____

5. What do Roy Rogers and Kenny Rogers have in common?

   _____

   Which one is the youngest?_____

   How much younger? _____ After reading their biographies, which man do you think has made the greatest contribution to the entertainment world?

   _____

   Why? _____

   _____

6. What is Leo Buscaglia's occupation? _____

   What nicknames has Dr. Buscaglia accumulated as he emerged as a national celebrity?_____

   What is one quote that Dr. Buscaglia is well known for which has to do with his wish for people? _____

   What does this mean to you?_____

   _____

   What did Dr. Buscaglia do to help himself ``look for me''?

   _____

   _____

The Dictionary

Study Guide

Directions: Using a dictionary, complete the following:

1. Name of reference book _____

2. What is a pronunciation key?_____
   Where is it found in the dictionary you are using?
   _____
   _____

3. Usually when a word has more than one definition, how is the decision made to determine the order in which the definitions are given?
   _____
   _____

4. What is the difference between an "abridged" and "unabridged" dictionary?
   _____
   _____

   Which type do you use in your classroom? _____
   In the library? _____

5. What is meant by the term "colloquialism"? _____
   _____

6. Do dictionaries give the etymologies of words? Explain.
   _____
   _____

7. What purpose do guide words serve?_____
   _____
   _____

8. Skim the pages of your dictionary that preceed the entry words and definitions. List the various types of information included.
   _____
   _____
   _____
   _____
   _____
   _____

The Dictionary

What Did You Uncover?

Directions: Upon completion of the activity sheet(s) assigned, answer the following:

1. What is the **main** function of a dictionary? _____
_____

2. List seven other things the dictionary contains other than words and their definitions? List these in the order in which they are the most valuable to you.

_____

_____

_____

_____

_____

_____

3. What did you find out about the dictionary that surprised you? _____
_____

760   relate | reliant

had a relapse. 1 *v.*, **re lapsed, re laps ing**; 2 *n.* —**re-
laps'er,** *n.*
re late (ri lāt'), **1** give an account of; tell: *The traveler
related her adventures.* **2** connect in thought or meaning:
"Better" and "best" are related to "good." **3** be connected
in any way: *We are interested in what relates to ourselves.*
v., **re lat ed, re lat ing.** [*Relate* is from Latin *relatum,*
meaning "brought back, related," which comes from *re-,*
meaning "back," and *latum,* meaning "brought."] —**re-
lat'er,** *n.*
re lat ed (ri lā'tid), **1** connected in any way. **2** belonging
to the same family; connected by a common origin:
Cousins are related. adj. —**re lat'ed ness,** *n.*
re la tion (ri lā'shən), **1** connection in thought or meaning: *Your answer has no relation to the question.*
2 connection by family ties of blood or marriage; relationship: *What relation are you to her?* **3** person who belongs to the same family as another; relative.
4 relations, *pl.* dealings between persons, groups, countries, etc.: *international relations. Our firm has business
relations with their firm.* **5** act of telling; account: *We
enjoyed the relation of the traveler's adventures. n.*
in relation to or **with relation to,** in reference to; in
regard to; about; concerning: *We must plan in relation to
the future.*
re la tion ship (ri lā'shən ship), **1** connection: *What is
the relationship of clouds to rain?* **2** condition of belonging
to the same family. *n.*
rel a tive (rel'ə tiv), **1** person who belongs to the same

2 take and carry farther: *relay a message.* **3** a relay race.
4 one part of a relay race. **5** an electromagnetic device
with a weak current which acts as a switch for a circuit
with a stronger current. Relays are used in equipment
for transmitting telegraph and telephone messages.
1,3-5 *n.*, 2 *v.*
re-lay (rē lā'), lay again: *That floor must be re-laid. v.*,
re-laid, re-lay ing.

relay race—The runner on the left is finishing his part of
the race. While still running, he hands a thin, metal rod
to his teammate on the right.

re lay race (rē'lā), race in which each member of a
team runs, swims, etc., only a certain part of the distance.

The Dictionary
Activity Sheet A

Directions: Using a dictionary, complete the following:

1. In each of the following pairs of words, circle the one which is spelled correctly:

   penicillin   lieutenant   rhinoceros   kaleidoscope

   penacillin   liutenant   rhinocerous   kalidoscope

2. Find the guide words for each of the following:

   jurisprudence   _____   _____

   horticulturist   _____   _____

   oblique   _____   _____

   apocalypse   _____   _____

   suffrage   _____   _____

3. If a person held legal claim upon the property of another, would he put a "lean" or a "lien" on the property? _____

4. Which officials would be most concerned with the actions of a "pyromaniac"?

   _____

5. What does a numismatist collect?

   _____

   A philatelist? _____

6. What different ways can the word "medieval" be pronounced?

   _____

7. Would you enjoy being a "lexicographer"? _____
   Why or why not? _____

   _____

   _____

8. Circle the word that fits in the following sentence:
   The shadow on the wall created an (allusion, illusion) of a giant monster.

The Dictionary

Activity Sheet B

Directions: Using a dictionary, complete the following:

1. Put a check in front of each sentence that is true.
   a. _____ I would prefer to be an anesthesiologist rather than an anarchist.
   b. _____ An adder cannot slither up trees.
   c. _____ A fathom is a measure of distance.
   d. _____ It is better to have a friend who is malevolent rather than magnanimous.

2. Give an example of a rhetorical question. _____
   _____

3. What do the following idioms mean? (Hint: look up key words.)

   A thorn in my side _____

   The guilt preyed on his conscience _____

4. Use each of the words below in a sentence. Make sure your sentence reflects an understanding of the definition. (Caution: some words may require a special word along with it.)

   penchant_____

   volition _____

5. Each of the following words has several forms. Find the definition for the part of speech listed next to each word.

   postulate (vt.)_____

   eclectic (n.)_____

6. From where did the following words originate and what do they mean?

   quixotic (see Don Quixote) _____
   _____
   _____

   narcissus (see Narcissus) _____
   _____
   _____

   tantalize (see Tantalus) _____
   _____
   _____

7. Give an example of a time in school when you found yourself in a "quagmire."
   _____
   _____

Encyclopedia of Careers and Vocational Guidance

Study Guide

Directions: Using the *Encyclopedia of Careers and Vocational Guidance,* answer the following:

1. Name of reference book _____

2. Fill in the following:

   Author/Editor _____

   Publisher _____

   Place of Publication_____

   Date of Publication _____

3. What is meant by the term "vocational guidance"? _____

   _____

   _____

4. What is the purpose of the *Encyclopedia of Careers and Vocational Guidance?*

   _____

   _____

5. What type of information is located in Volume I? _____

   _____

   What type of information is located in Volume II?_____

   _____

6. Imagine that you are interested in pursuing a career in journalism. Describe how you would locate information on that field in Volume I?

   _____

   _____

   _____

   In Volume II? _____

   _____

7. How can the bibliography "Books of Additional Information" be useful?

   _____

   _____

   _____

   How is it organized? _____

Encyclopedia of Careers and Vocational Guidance

Study Guide Continued

8. What information does the "List of Colleges and Universities" contain?

_____

_____

9. Volume II begins with "Occupational Listing with Government Classification." Explain how this list can help you gather additional information on a specific career. _____

_____

_____

What Did You Uncover?

Directions: Upon completion of the activity sheet(s) assigned, answer the following:

1. Why is the term "Encyclopedia" in the title an accurate one to use?

_____

_____

2. Describe the type of people who would most benefit from the *Encyclopedia of Careers and Vocational Guidance* and explain how the reference book could be of value to each.

_____

_____

_____

3. If you were to create an advertisement for the *Encyclopedia of Careers and Vocational Guidance* what three things about this reference book would you be sure to include? (List them in order of importance to you.)

_____

_____

_____

Encyclopedia of Careers and Vocational Guidance

Activity Sheet A

Directions: Using the *Encyclopedia of Careers and Vocational Guidance*, complete the following:

1. In Volume I, for each career field mentioned, a brief paragraph gives a summary of the career. Locate the section on "The Advertising Business." In your **own** words, describe the advertising business.

   _____

   _____

2. Read a career field article in Volume I under the subject "Retailing," and list the related articles it suggests you look up in Volume II.

   _____

   _____

3. If you are not a good athlete but want a career in sports, what type of jobs might be available?_____

   _____

4. How would a person interested in getting a job as an interpreter enter the field?

   _____

   What is the "Employment Outlook" for this profession?

   _____

5. As in most careers, the educational or vocational training fulfills only part of the requirements. There are other special requirements that can not be taught. What "Special Requirements" must a person meet to become an Air Traffic Controller?

   _____

6. Choose a broad career field in Volume I that you would like to research. What is this broad career field?

   _____

   What related article(s) does Volume I list?

   _____

   Read the related article(s) in Volume II. What career within this field seems to best suit your personality, talents, etc.?

   _____

   Explain your answer. _____

Encyclopedia of Careers and Vocational Guidance

Activity Sheet B

Directions: Using the *Encyclopedia of Careers and Vocational Guidance*, complete the following:

1. Skim through the articles in Volume I that preceed the "Career Fields" portion. What is the title of the article you find most interesting and informative?

   _____

   Summarize the main points of this article. _____

   _____

   _____

   _____

2. In what ways has the computer industry changed over the past few years?

   _____

   _____

   What conditions have led to this change? _____

   _____

   What type of jobs are available in the field of computer technology today?

   _____

   _____

3. Compare the "Requirements" and "Nature of the Work" among optometrists, opticians, and ophthalmologists.

   _____

   _____

   _____

   Of the three, which would you choose to be? _____

   Explain your answer. _____

   _____

4. If you were interviewing a person who was considering a job with the FBI, what questions would you ask? (Base questions on the information you've learned in the *Encyclopedia of Careers and Vocational Guidance.*)

   _____

   _____

   _____

   _____

From *Unlocking the Secrets of Research*, Copyright © 1986 Scott, Foresman and Company

Encyclopedia of Careers and Vocational Guidance

Activity Sheet B Continued

5. Choose a career that is held by a favorite relative. What is the career?

_____

Complete the chart below by locating information concerning this career today, and by interviewing this relative to learn what the job was like when he/she first began.

Career Name		
	Today	Yesterday
Beginning Salary		
Job Requirements		
Job Conditions		
Employment Opportunities		

6. Skim through Volume II. What jobs are available today which were not available twenty years ago?

_____

_____

Other than the fact that there are always different career possibilities, why is it important to use a recently published volume of the *Encyclopedia of Careers and Vocational Guidance?*_____

_____

7. Look at the "Help Wanted" column in your local newspaper. What things are usually included in each ad?

_____

_____

8. Imagine that you own a fast-food restaurant and need a chef to prepare the food. Create a "Help Wanted" ad for this job. Write it on the back of this page.

Name _____ *Date* _____

Famous First Facts

Study Guide

Directions: Using the book *Famous First Facts,* complete the following:

1. Name of reference book _____

2. Fill in the following information:

   Author/Editor _____

   Publisher _____

   Place of Publication _____

   Date of Publication _____

3. List the types of indexes included in *Famous First Facts* and explain how each is organized.

   _____

   _____

   _____

   _____

4. How are the entries in *Famous First Facts* arranged?

   _____

5. Often you will locate certain facts only when you look up the main subject under which it would fall. For example, if you wanted to know the name of the first asteroid named for an American President, or how the first meteoric display (shooting stars) on record was described, you would have to look under the general category of ''Astronomy.''

   List three subheadings listed under the general category ''Telephone.''

   _____

   _____

   _____

6. It will often be necessary to do detective work before locating the facts you need. For example, if you wanted to learn first facts relating to the subject of ''Comic Books'' you would be told under the entry ''Comic Books'' to ''See Periodical; Comic Books.'' You would then look up ''Periodicals'' and then locate the subheading ''Comic Books.''

   List two other subjects that direct you to ''See...'' another more general category and tell what that category is.

   _____ See_____

   _____ See_____

20   From *Unlocking the Secrets of Research,* Copyright © 1986 Scott, Foresman and Company

Famous First Facts

Study Guide Continued

7. When using the "Names Index" you will find the "famous first fact" relating to each individual. In the darker letters are the categories in which you can find more information.

   Look up Richard Byrd. List two categories in which you could locate additional information about him.

   _____

   _____

   _____

What Did You Uncover?

Directions: Upon completion of the activity sheet(s) assigned, answer the following:

1. *Famous First Facts* gives information that can be found in general encyclopedias. Why, then, is it considered an important resource tool when doing research?

   _____

   _____

2. Of all the "famous firsts" that you discovered while using *Famous First Facts,* which did you find most significant?

   _____

   _____

   Which did you find most humorous? _____

   _____

3. How far back (to what year) does *Famous First Facts* go? _____

Famous First Facts

Activity Sheet A

Directions: Using the book of *Famous First Facts*, complete the following:

1. For what "famous firsts" is Amelia Earhart remembered? _____
   _____
   _____

2. By what name were the first bicycles known?_____

3. How did the Ferris Wheel get its name? _____
   _____

   When was it first displayed?_____

4. Describe the first electronic computer—ENIAC._____
   _____
   _____

   How did it compare with the first solid-state electronic computer built twelve years later?
   _____
   _____

5. Impeachment proceedings were first instituted against which U.S. President?
   _____

   How close did he come to actually being impeached? _____
   _____

6. What famous inventor put Menlo Park, New Jersey, on the map?_____
   _____

   What "famous first" was invented there? _____

7. Look up the month and day of your birthday. What "famous firsts" are listed for that day?
   _____
   _____
   _____

   Did any of them actually happen on the exact day (including year) in which you were born? _____ If so, which one(s)?
   _____

8. How was the first piano different from the ones we use today? _____
   _____
   _____

Famous First Facts

Activity Sheet B

Directions: Using the book of *Famous First Facts,* complete the following:

1. Who received the Nobel Peace Prize on December 10, 1950? _____

   _____

   List three ways you can find this information using *Famous First Facts.*

   _____

   _____

   _____

2. It has been said that, ''Necessity is the Mother of Invention.'' Would this saying be appropriate for helping to explain how the first ice cream cone originated?
   _____ Why or why not?_____

   _____

3. What events did the first U.S. commemorative postage stamps depict? _____

   _____

   What famous U.S. event would you like to see immortalized? _____

   _____

   Draw your own commemorative stamp to depict this.

4. In the ''Geographical Index'', find a city listed that is closest to the one in which you live. (Use a map to help you if necessary.) Name the city.

   _____

   For what ''famous firsts'' is this city known? _____

   _____

5. Look up the year in which you were born. Choose one ''famous first'' that occured in that year that you believe is the most important. Describe this ''famous first'' and explain why you think it is so important.

   _____

   _____

Name _____  Date _____

Guinness Book of World Records

Study Guide

Directions: Using the *Guinness Book of World Records,* complete the following:

1. Name of book _____

2. Fill in the following information:

   Author/Editor _____

   Publisher _____

   Place of Publication _____

   Date of Publication _____

3. What is the major purpose of this reference book?

   _____

   _____

4. How did the *Guinness Book of World Records* originate?_____

   _____

   _____

5. How do the publishers determine what records to publish in the *Guinness Book of World Records?*

   _____

   _____

   _____

6. What are at least six categories for which records are given?

   _____

   _____

   _____

7. How does someone document and validate that a record has been established?

   _____

   _____

   _____

8. How do you locate information in the *Guinness Book of World Records?* _____

   _____

   _____

   _____

Guinness Book of World Records

What Did You Uncover?

Directions: After completion of the activity sheet(s) assigned, answer the following:

1. What suggestions would you make to the publishers in regard to the next publication of the *Guinness Book of World Records?*

   _____

   _____

   _____

   _____

2. What did you find to be the most helpful in locating information in this book?

   _____

   _____

   _____

   Least helpful? _____

   _____

   _____

3. Do you think that the information provided in the *Guinness Book of World Records* is important or not?

   _____

   Why or why not? _____

   _____

   _____

Guinness Book of World Records

Activity Sheet A

Directions: Using the *Guinness Book of World Records*, complete the following:

1. Which took longer, a man eating 100 yards of spaghetti or a man circling the bases on a baseball field?

   _____

   What was the difference in time? _____

2. What three televised events attracted the most viewers nationwide? _____

   _____

   _____

   _____

   Did you view any of these events? _____

   If so, describe the event. _____

   _____

3. Of all the records established in the *Guinness Book of World Records*, which one would you like to challenge or break?

   _____

   Why? _____

4. Which is the most expensive, a pound of great cheese or a pound of delicious chocolates?

   _____

   What is the difference in cost? _____

   What is the name of the world's most expensive cheese? _____

   What is the name of the most expensive chocolate? _____

5. When was the earliest public demonstration of television given? _____

   When was the first television broadcasting service opened? _____

   How many television sets received this first broadcast? _____

   Had there been any previous attempts for broadcasting service? _____

   Explain. _____

   _____

From *Unlocking the Secrets of Research*, Copyright © 1986 Scott, Foresman and Company

Guinness Book of World Records

Activity Sheet B

Directions: Using the Guinness Book of World Records, complete the following:

1. What are at least two records you would like to see included in the *Guinness Book of World Records* that are not included?

   _____

   _____

   Why would these be important to include? _____

   _____

2. What kind of gluttony (eating/drinking) records will the *Guinness Book of World Records* not include?

   _____

   _____

   Why will they not include such records? _____

   _____

   Do you agree or disagree with this position? _____

   Why or why not? _____

   _____

3. What country has the lowest average age for marriage for females? _____

   _____

   What country has the highest average age for marriage for females? _____

   _____

   What is this age?_____ How does this compare with the overall youngest and oldest ages for voting?

   _____

4. What is the largest contract ever paid to a TV star?_____

   To whom was this paid? _____

   Is this more or less than the highest price ever paid for a painting? _____

   What was the name of the painting and the artist? _____

   _____

Guinness Book of World Records

Activity Sheet B Continued

5. Write a brief paragraph about one record from the *Guinness Book of World Records* in which you are most interested. Include details of this record (i.e. age, duration, time, expense, etc.) and tell why you chose this record.

_____

_____

_____

6. What record, set by a woman, do you feel is most interesting and/or significant?

_____

By a man? _____

By a child (under eighteen)? _____

_____

7. If you wanted to live in the smallest independent country in the world, where would you live?

_____

What is the population of this country? _____

According to the statistics given, do you feel the population of this country will increase? _____ Why or why not?

_____

8. Of all the human achievement records set, which three do you think are the most amazing?

_____

_____

_____

Which three do you think are the most significant?

_____

_____

_____

The Thesaurus

Study Guide

Directions: Using a thesaurus, complete the following:

1. Name of reference book _____

2. Fill in the following information:

   Author/Editor _____

   Publisher _____

   Place of Publication_____

   Date of Publication _____

3. What is the definition of a thesaurus? _____

   _____

4. A synonym can be described as meaning, "almost but not quite." Explain this definition of a synonym.

   _____

5. A thesaurus can be organized in different ways. Locate two thesauruses that are organized differently. Describe the method you would use in each to find a synonym for a certain word.

   _____

   _____

   _____

What Did You Uncover?

Directions: Upon completion of the activity sheet(s) assigned, answer the following:

1. How does a thesaurus differ from a dictionary? _____

   _____

   _____

2. How can a thesaurus improve your writing ability? _____

   _____

   _____

The Thesaurus

What Did You Uncover? Continued

3. List three different things a thesaurus includes. _____
   _____
   _____
   _____

4. When choosing a word from those listed as synonyms in a thesaurus, what must you be careful to remember?
   _____
   _____

changeable *Changeable* means able or likely to change. The weather has been so *changeable* that I don't know whether to take sunglasses or an umbrella with me today. *Changeable* is often used to describe a person who jumps from one opinion or attitude to another. Jan is very *changeable*—one day she likes her new house and the next day she doesn't.

iridescent *Iridescent* describes something that shows changing colors. A fountain sometimes looks *iridescent* when it has the colors of the rainbow in it. A soap bubble can be described as *iridescent*.

reversible *Reversible* means able to move backward and forward or able to be turned around. A *reversible* coat has two sides that can be used as the outside.

fickle *Fickle* means often changeable without much reason. A *fickle* friend is not really a friend at all, because he or she may turn away from you at any time. He is so *fickle*—one day he's friendly and the next day he's not.

The Thesaurus

Activity Sheet A

Directions: Using a thesaurus, complete the following:

1. Select a magazine advertisement and attach it to this page. Underline all the adjectives and verbs. Then, rewrite the advertisement using the thesaurus to find a **different** word for those you've underlined.

   _____

   _____

   _____

   _____

   _____

   _____

2. The word "said" is one of the most overused of all words. List all the words you can find to substitute for the word "said."

   _____

   _____

   _____

3. Suppose you were assigned to write a paragraph to describe an ordinary object—such as a spoon. Use the thesaurus to help make your paragraph anything but ordinary. (You can write your paragraph on the subject of a spoon or any other ordinary object.)

   _____

   _____

   _____

   _____

   _____

   _____

4. List five words that could be used to replace the word "anger" in the sentence, "As the day progressed, I could feel my 'anger' at his insensitivity grow."

   _____

   _____

   _____

The Thesaurus

Activity Sheet A Continued

5. Words carry degrees of mildness or strength. For example, the word ''anger'' is not as strong as the word ''rage.'' Using the words you found for item #4, list the synonyms according to the degree of feeling they evoke.

    Weakest _____

    _____

    _____

    _____

    Strongest _____

6. Using the thesaurus, describe your version of a space scene as vividly as possible. Choose words which will allow the reader to ''see'' the scene without actually seeing it.

    _____

    _____

    _____

    _____

    _____

    _____

    _____

    _____

7. The word ''broke'' is a slang term to describe people who are in a state of poverty. List more formal words for the word ''broke.''

    _____   _____

    _____   _____

8. List as many ''color words'' as you can find to describe the sky from sunrise to sunset.

    _____   _____

    _____   _____

    _____   _____

    _____   _____

    _____   _____

    _____   _____

Name _____  Date _____

The Thesaurus

Activity Sheet B

Directions: Using a thesaurus, complete the following:

1. If you were to define the word "right" to a person from another country it would be quite difficult since there are so many different meanings for this word. Give three synonyms that would help to explain three different uses of the word "right."

   _____

   _____

2. Find three synonyms and two antonyms for the word "vociferous."

   synonyms _____ _____ _____

   antonyms _____ _____ _____

3. The words "imply" and "insinuate" are listed in the thesaurus as synonyms for the word "suggest;" yet, there is a shade of difference between them. Illustrate the difference by using each word in a sentence.

   imply_____

   insinuate _____

4. Select a news article that you find interesting and attach it to this page. Underline the common nouns (i.e. car, laughter, house, book, etc.). Then, rewrite one paragraph from the article using the thesaurus to find a **different** word for those you've underlined.

   _____

   _____

   _____

   _____

   _____

   _____

   _____

5. Choose five words you find yourself using over and over again. On the back of this sheet list ten words for each that can be used instead.

   _____ _____ _____

   _____ _____

6. Words have been described as hackneyed. Read a few pages from a favorite fiction book and identify ten words that you feel are hackneyed. On the back of this sheet list these ten words and give two other words which are more interesting for each.

From *Unlocking the Secrets of Research,* Copyright © 1986 Scott, Foresman and Company

Name _____  Date _____

Twentieth Century Authors

Study Guide

Directions: Using *Twentieth Century Authors*, complete the following:

1. Name of reference book _____

2. Author/Editor _____

   Publisher _____

   Place of publication _____

   Date of publication _____

3. What criteria is used to determine which writers are included in *Twentieth Century Authors?*

   _____

   _____

   _____

4. Place a check (✔) on the line next to those authors who would **not** be included in *Twentieth Century Authors*. Next to those names you have checked, explain **why** they aren't included. (If you are unfamiliar with those not included in *Twentieth Century Authors*, you might consult another reference book for aid.)

   _____ William Shakespeare _____

   _____ Mark Twain _____

   _____ Sinclair Lewis _____

   _____ Miguel de Cervantes_____

   _____ Walt Whitman _____

   _____ Edgar Allan Poe _____

   _____ George Orwell _____

5. What general type of information is included in each biographical sketch?

   _____

   _____

6. Would you consider *Twentieth Century Authors* to be biographical, autobiographical, or both? _____

   Explain. _____

   _____

   _____

Name _____  Date _____

Twentieth Century Authors

What Did You Uncover?

Directions: Upon completion of the activity sheet(s) assigned, answer the following:

1. Since *Twentieth Century Authors* contains no indexes, how is information located?

   _____

   _____

   _____

2. What type of indexes would you like to see included in *Twentieth Century Authors*?

   _____

   _____

   _____

3. If you want to do further research on an author you've looked up in *Twentieth Century Authors,* how can the book be of further aid?

   _____

   _____

   _____

4. In your opinion, what is the greatest contribution of *Twentieth Century Authors*?

   _____

   _____

   _____

   _____

Twentieth Century Authors

Activity Sheet A

Directions: Using *Twentieth Century Authors,* complete the following:

1. Edgar Rice Burroughs is best remembered for his book about a boy brought up among the apes in Africa. Who is this famous hero?

   _____

   _____

   Burroughs also wrote a series of stories about life on which planet?

   _____

2. Agatha Christie wrote of the many people who encouraged her to write. Based on her recollections, which person do you think had the most influence upon her career?

   _____

   Explain your answer. _____
   What **type** of book is she best known for writing?_____
   List three principal works by Agatha Christie. _____

   _____

   _____

3. From where did Sinclair Lewis get his inspiration for his book *Main Street?*

   _____

   What awards did he receive? _____
   List two other sources you could consult that would include information on Sinclair Lewis.

   _____

   _____

4. What type of jobs did Robert Frost hold? _____

   _____

   Frost has been compared to which great English poet(s)?_____

   _____

   Complete Frost's description of a poem, ''A poem begins in delight and ends...''

   _____

   Give your own definition of a poem. _____

   _____

Twentieth Century Authors

Activity Sheet A Continued

5. Where did Will Rogers say he learned everything he knew? _____
_____

Do you think this is true of people your age?_____ Where do you learn most of the things you know?

_____

What honors were posthumously bestowed upon Rogers? _____
_____

6. Many of the world's greatest writers did not receive rave reviews right away. What did Sax Rohmer do with his letters of reject?

_____

_____

How do you think you would handle similar rejections from publishers? _____
_____

7. To young children everywhere, who is Theodore Geisel?_____
_____

How did he develop this pen name? _____
_____

List three things about this remarkable man that you think others might be interested to learn?

_____

_____

_____

8. What is one of your favorite books?_____
Who wrote it?_____
Is this author located in *Twentieth Century Authors*? _____
If not, why do you think this author is not included? _____
_____

If so, list three interesting facts about the author. _____

_____

_____

_____

Twentieth Century Authors

Activity Sheet B

Directions: Using *Twentieth Century Authors*, complete the following:

1. What is a pseudonym? _____

   What was the pseudonym used by William Sydney Porter?_____

   If you were asked to sum up the life of William Sydney Porter in three sentences, what would you write?

   _____

   _____

   _____

2. From what experiences did Rudyard Kipling draw when writing the book *Kim*?

   _____

   _____

   Which books and poems by Kipling are you familiar with? List them and write a brief summary of each.

   _____

   _____

   _____

3. What American president was the subject of a six volume biography by Carl Sandburg?

   _____

   Why was Sandburg awarded the Pulitzer Prize for history rather than for writing a biography?

   _____

   _____

   If you were to do further research on Sandburg, which references listed would you select?

   _____

   _____

4. Who were the authors behind the pseudonym Ellery Queen?_____

   _____

   Ellery Queen, the hero of their books, was involved in what profession?

   _____

From *Unlocking the Secrets of Research*, Copyright © 1986 Scott, Foresman and Company

Twentieth Century Authors

Activity Sheet B Continued

What do you consider to be an advantage to writing under a pseudonym?

_____

What do you consider to be a disadvantage to writing under a pseudonym?

_____

5. What was so remarkable or unusual about the life of William Henry Davies? (How did he spend his earlier years compared to the years after thirty?)

_____

_____

Name the autobiography for which he is famous. _____

From what you have read about Davies, would you be interested in reading such an autobiography? _____

Explain your answer. _____

_____

6. Based on the information in *Twentieth Century Authors,* compare and contrast the lives and works of William Faulkner and John Steinbeck.

_____

_____

_____

_____

_____

_____

_____

7. What is one of your favorite poems? _____

Who wrote it? _____

Is this author listed in *Twentieth Century Authors?* _____

If not, why do you think this author is not included? _____

_____

If so, list three interesting facts about the author. _____

_____

_____

_____

Webster's Biographical Dictionary

Study Guide

Directions: Using *Webster's Biographical Dictionary* complete the following:

1. Name of reference book _____

2. Author/Editor _____

   Publisher _____

   Place of Publication _____

   Date of Publication _____

3. Why is *Webster's Biographical* classified as a ``dictionary''?

   _____

   _____

   _____

4. How does *Webster's Biographical Dictionary* differ from a regular dictionary?

   _____

   _____

5. What do the following abbreviations in *Webster's Biographical Dictionary* represent? Next to each, explain what the term means:

   colloq. _____

   anon. _____

   obs. _____

6. Skim through the tables included in *Webster's Biographical Dictionary*. List three tables and describe each.

   _____

   _____

   _____

7. Why have certain entries been included in the ``addenda'' rather than in the main body of *Webster's Biographical Dictionary?*

   _____

   _____

   _____

Webster's Biographical Dictionary

What Did You Uncover?

Directions: Upon completion of the activity sheet(s) assigned, answer the following:

1. How would you define a "*Biographical Dictionary*"? _____
   _____
   _____
   _____

2. Since the information in *Webster's Biographical Dictionary* is fairly brief, how can this reference book be helpful to you in your research?
   _____
   _____
   _____

3. In the preface to *Webster's Biographical Dictionary*, the reader is asked for criticisms and/or suggestions to improve the dictionary. What suggestions might you send the editors?
   _____
   _____
   _____
   _____

Webster's Biographical Dictionary

Activity Sheet A

Directions: Using *Webster's Biographical Dictionary*, complete the following:

1. What do the *original* Engelbert Humperdinck and Engelbert Humperdinck, the modern singer, have in common?

   _____

   _____

   What is the *original* Engelbert Humperdinck best known for composing?

   _____

   What connection was there between the first Engelbert Humperdinck and William Shakespeare?

   _____

   _____

2. Who was Plato's famous teacher? _____

   For what crimes was his teacher imprisoned?_____

   _____

   How was Plato instrumental in helping the world remember his teacher?

   _____

3. What three men served as Chief Justice of the U.S. Supreme Court during the administration of George Washington?

   _____

   _____

   Why was John Rutledge's term so brief?

   _____

4. What were the two main subject matters for the paintings and sculptures of Frederic Remington?

   _____

   _____

   What other professions did he pursue? _____

   _____

5. What was Confucius' real name and what does this name mean?

   _____

   What is the *Analects*?_____

   _____

Webster's Biographical Dictionary

Activity Sheet B

Directions: Using *Webster's Biographical Dictionary*, complete the following:

1. What cause did Thomas Paine's publication, *Common Sense,* aid? _____
_____

   Why was Paine outlawed from England? _____

   Based on the information in *Webster's Biographical Dictionary,* what were Paine's views on democracy?
_____

_____

2. How did the Merriam family become involved in publishing dictionaries?
_____

   When was the first *Merriam-Webster Dictionary* published? _____

3. When and by whom was the "Hall of Fame for Great Americans" established?
_____

   List three inventors chosen for this honor. _____
_____

   List three statesmen chosen. _____
_____

   What great American, not yet chosen, would you select to be included in the "Hall of Fame"?
_____

   Under which category would this person belong? _____

4. What book tells of the adventures that Lewis and Clark experienced during their famous expedition?
_____

_____

   Who was responsible for writing this book? _____

5. The statue of Horatio Nelson stands at Trafalgar Square in London, England. Why is it so fitting for this statue to be located where it is?
_____

_____

Webster's Biographical Dictionary

Activity Sheet B Continued

In **one** sentence, based on the information you have located in *Webster's Biographical Dictionary*, describe Horatio Nelson.

_____

_____

6. What do Benjamin Rush, Thomas Jefferson, and George Wythe have in common?

_____

List four others who are also famous for the same thing. _____

_____

7. Who became Poet Laureate of England after the death of William Wordsworth?

_____

For how many years did he (Wordsworth's successor) hold this honor? _____

Which of his poems deals with King Arthur and the Arthurian legend?

_____

8. Under what pseudonym did Benjamin Franklin publish *Poor Richard's Almanac*?

_____

Based on the information given, list the three accomplishments of Benjamin Franklin that you feel are most valuable.

_____

_____

_____

9. For what contribution was Susan B. Anthony best known?_____

_____

Who were her coauthors of *History of Woman Suffrage?*_____

10. By what term was Florence Nightingale known? _____

_____

Given only the information in *Webster's Biographical Dictionary*, why is this term so appropriate?

_____

_____

Who's Who in America

Study Guide

Directions: Using *Who's Who In America*, complete the following:

1. Name of reference book _____

2. Author/Editor _____

   Publisher _____

   Place of Publication _____

   Date of Publication _____

   Edition _____

3. What is the purpose of *Who's Who In America?* _____
   _____

4. What are three other Who's Who books that are published by the Marquis Who's Who, Inc.?
   _____
   _____

5. What is the purpose of the Board of Advisors? _____
   _____

6. How do you find someone's name in *Who's Who in America?* _____
   _____

   What if someone has a compound hyphenated surname? _____
   _____

7. Many abbreviations are used in the biographies. How can you find out what these abbreviations mean?
   _____
   _____

8. When you are reading a biography you will find that, in addition to abbreviations, there are a lot of numbers, dates, names, etc. How do you know what these things mean?
   _____
   _____

   What type of information is provided about the biographees?
   _____
   _____
   _____

Who's Who In America

Study Guide Continued

9. There are several different kinds of indexes found in *Who's Who In America*. One is the "Retiree Index." Where is the "Retiree Index" located?

_____

What information does the "Retiree Index" provide? _____

What is the "Necrology Index"? _____

Where is this index located? _____

What other index(es) are provided? _____

_____

What Did You Uncover?

Directions: Upon completion of the activity sheet(s) assigned, complete the following:

1. What did you like least about *Who's Who In America*? _____

_____

What did you like best about *Who's Who In America*? _____

_____

2. Do you agree with the publisher's selection of people to be listed in *Who's Who In America*? _____ Why or why not?

_____

_____

3. What criteria for the selection of biographies to *Who's Who In America* did you feel were most valid?

_____

_____

Name _____ Date _____

Who's Who In America

Activity Sheet A

Directions: Using *Who's Who In America*, complete the following:

1. Look at the occupations of all the Browns listed. What occupation appears to be the most predominant?

   _____

   Which occupation seems the most unusual to you? _____

   Were there any occupations you had never heard of? _____ If so, which ones?

   _____

   In which of these occupations would you most like to be involved?

   _____

2. Look up your surname in *Who's Who In America*. (If you can't find your surname, look for a friend's surname. Keep looking until you find a surname that is the same as some-one you know.) How many entries did you find with this surname? _____ By reading the information provided, which person do you think you'd most likely want to meet?

   _____

   Why? _____

   _____

   Note: If only one person is listed, then tell if you'd like to meet that person and why or why not.

3. Look at all the Andersons listed in the *Who's Who In America*.. Which one is the oldest?

   _____

   Which one is the youngest? _____

   Which one has the most children? _____

4. Think of a person that you admire and respect who is well-known. Find out if that person is listed in *Who's Who In America*. If listed, write a brief paragraph telling about that person. If the person is not listed, tell why you think he/she may have been overlooked?

   _____

   _____

   _____

5. Where do the publishers get the information published in *Who's Who In America*?

   _____

   _____

   How can you tell from which of these sources the information was obtained?

   _____

   _____

Who's Who In America

Activity Sheet B

Directions: Using *Who's Who In America,* complete the following:

1. Marital information is provided for each biographee. What information is provided if the person has been married more than one time?

   _____

   List three biographees that have been married more than one time.

   _____

   _____

2. Some biographies have statements written in italics following the data presented. Peruse the book and read at least ten of these statements and the data provided about the person. Write the name of the person you selected and copy one statement about this person.

   _____

   _____

   _____

   _____

   _____

   Why did you select this statement? _____

   _____

   Did anything in the biographical data affect your selection? _____

   If so, what? _____

3. Using the "Key to Information in this Directory" as a guideline for what information to include in a biography for *Who's Who In America.* Interview an adult, gather the information necessary to write a biography, and then write a biography that could be submitted to *Who's Who in America.*

   _____

   _____

   _____

   _____

   _____

   _____

   _____

   _____

   _____

   _____

Who's Who In America

Activity Sheet B Continued

4. Look through the biographies for people by the name of Davis. Find all those that are listed as educators. How many did you find? _____
Of these educators, what conclusions can you make in regard to the professional organization to which they belong?

_____

_____

From what you read about them, why do you think they are listed in *Who's Who In America*.

_____

_____

5. What considerations are given in selecting nominees for *Who's Who In America?*

_____

_____

6. Choose an occupation that is of interest to you. What occupation did you choose?

_____

Peruse *Who's Who In America* and read at least twenty biographies (or as many as are available) of people who have that occupation. Which one of these people do you think **most** deserves the honor of being listed in this publication?

_____

Why? _____

_____

If you had to make a decision and eliminate one of the people you just read about who would it be?

_____

Why? _____

_____

_____

World Almanac

Study Guide

Directions: Using an almanac, complete the following:

1. Name of reference book _____

2. Fill in the following information:

   Publisher _____

   Place of Publication_____

   Date of Publication _____

3. Where does the publisher get the information that is published in the almanac?

   _____

   _____

4. What is the purpose of the almanac?_____

   _____

   _____

5. Give examples of five kinds of information that may be found in an almanac.

   _____

   _____

   _____

   _____

   _____

6. How is the information in the almanac kept current? _____

   _____

   _____

7. How do you locate information in an almanac?

   _____

   _____

8. If you wish to find additional information on the data presented, how might you do it?

   _____

   _____

   _____

World Almanac

What Did You Uncover?

Directions: Upon completion of the activity sheet(s) assigned, answer the following

1. What information in the almanac did you think was the most interesting?
   _____
   _____
   _____

2. Now that you are familiar with the almanac, what information does it provide that you feel will be the most helpful to you?
   _____
   _____
   _____

3. What information is not included in the almanac that you would like to see included?
   _____
   _____
   _____
   _____

Name _____  *Date* _____

World Almanac

Activity Sheet A

Directions: Using an almanac, complete the following:

1. Of all the states, which have the highest rate per 100,000 for the following crimes:

   Murder _____

   Robbery _____

   Auto Theft _____

2. In 1981, was more national income in the U.S. made in transportation (water) or agriculture (farm)? _____ What was the difference in income?

   _____

3. If you wanted to break the 1984 men's Olympic records for the following events, what times would you need to beat?

   100 meter run _____

   1000 meter speed skating_____

   200 meter freestyle swimming _____

4. If friends asked you to travel with them to a state in the Union nicknamed the Beaver State, to which state would you be traveling?

   _____

   What three tourist attractions would you want to visit while you were there?

   _____

   _____

   _____

   What vegetables would you expect to find growing in this state?

   _____

5. If you mailed an air parcel that weighed 18 ounces from the United States to Greece, how much would it cost?_____ From U.S. to Vietnam? _____
   What are the restrictions for the size of packages?

   _____

   _____

   _____

Name _____  Date _____

World Almanac

Activity Sheet B

Directions: Using an almanac, complete the following:

1. In the years listed below, on what day of the week will July 14 fall?

   1899 _____   2000 _____

   1990 _____   2015 _____

   In the years listed below, on what day of the week did December 25 fall?

   1817 _____   1948 _____

   1893 _____   2080 _____

2. If you had $2500 dollars you wanted to invest in savings, what are at least three options you would have?

   _____

   _____

   _____

   Which do you feel would be the best investment for you? _____

   Why, what would be the benefits? _____

   _____

3. If you were training to be a boxer and your trainer said you had to eat the Recommended Daily Dietary Allowance of protein, how many grams of protein would you need to eat?_____ Circle three of the following foods that would be a good source of protein:

   sour cream   grapefruit   chicken   cabbage.

   saltine crackers   cottage cheese   lima beans

4. If it is 12:00 noon Eastern Standard Time in Miami, Florida, what time is it in San Francisco, California? _____ Wichita, Kansas? _____ Nome, Alaska? _____ London, England? _____

   What is meant by 18:00? _____

   How is standard time determined? _____

   _____

5. Guess who I am. I was a famous baseball player. I lived from 1896-1963. My last name began with an H. I was a National League second baseman. I twice won the triple crown. What's my name?_____

53

World Almanac

Activity Sheet B Continued

6. If you wished to move to a city that had the most recorded annual snowfall, where would you move?

_____

How many inches of snow did this city have?_____

Who are some famous people who have lived in this state? _____

_____

7. Which state has the highest per capita income? _____

What was the per capita income for this state in 1982? _____

Was it the highest per capita state in 1970? _____ Why do you think this state may have such a high per capita income?

_____

_____

8. From the list of "Entertainment Personalities," find one entertainer you like. What is his/her name?

_____

Where was this entertainer born? _____

On what date? _____ Why did you choose this entertainer?

_____

_____

Look over the list of "Original Names of Selected Entertainers." Is your entertainer listed there?_____ If so, what was his/her original name?

_____

9. Which of the following cities has the most hospitals: Phoenix, Arizona or Honolulu, Hawaii?

_____

How do these two cities compare in population? _____

What conclusions might you make about the hospitals in these two cities based on the facts you have?

_____

_____

_____

_____

Name _____  Date _____

World Atlas

Study Guide

Directions: Using an atlas, complete the following:

1. Name of reference book _____

2. Fill in the following information:

   Author/Editor _____

   Publisher _____

   Place of Publication_____

   Date of Publication _____

3. List ten different types of information that are found in this reference book.

   _____

   _____

   _____

4. What are latitude lines?_____

   Longitude lines? _____

   How are latitude and longitude lines helpful when using an atlas? _____

   _____

   _____

5. What information is provided in the atlas which will help you locate a particular city such as Lusaka?

   _____

   _____

6. Using the atlas, how can you determine distances from one point to another point?

   _____

   _____

7. What does an atlas provide that allows you to know if the land is mountainous, flat, hilly, etc.?

   _____

   _____

Name _____  Date _____

World Atlas

What Did You Uncover?

Directions: Upon completion of the activity sheet(s) assigned, answer the following:

1. Do you think the atlas is an important reference book? _____ Why or why not?

   _____

   _____

   _____

2. What information found in the atlas is most beneficial to you?

   _____

   Why? _____

   _____

3. To what groups of people would the atlas be especially beneficial?

   _____

   _____

   _____

   Why? _____

   _____

   _____

   _____

World Atlas

Activity Sheet A

Directions: Using an atlas, complete the following:

1. If you were sailing from Italy to Yugoslavia, what sea would you cross?

_____

If you wanted to sail from one coastal city of Italy to the closest coastal city of Yugoslavia, what would be your city of departure?

_____

Destination city? _____

2. If you wanted to live in a climate that was always hot, list five countries you would choose.

_____

_____

_____

3. Locate the vegetation map. Locate and then list four major states in the U.S. that have broadleaf deciduous trees.

_____

_____

What are two European countries that have similar natural vegetation?

_____

_____

4. If you were flying directly from Port Gentil, Gabon to Johannesburg, South Africa, what countries would you fly over?

_____

_____

What type of terrain would you expect to be flying over?

_____

_____

5. What three major bodies of water surround the United States?

_____

_____

6. Give an example of one location, country, or state where each of the following predominant economics could be found:

Fishing_____ Mining _____

▼

World Atlas

Activity Sheet A Continued

Nomadic Herding _____   Manufacturing and

Forestry _____   Commerce _____

7. What is the leading country or state in the production of each of the following?

Wheat _____

Tea _____

Rye _____

Coffee _____

Oats _____

Corn _____

Rice _____

Cane Sugar _____

Tobacco _____

Pineapples _____

8. If you were flying from Seattle, Washington to Miami, Florida, and you wanted to take the most direct route, what major cities would you go through?

_____

_____

9. Which of the following countries have the greatest annual rainfall? Circle one.

Poland   Yugoslavia   Tunisia

What type vegetation would you expect to find there?

_____

What conclusion can you draw about the effect of rainfall on vegetation?

_____

_____

Name _____  Date _____

World Atlas

Activity Sheet B

Directions: Using an atlas, complete the following:

1. What small island is located at 9.40 S. latitude and 158.00 W. longitude?

   _____

2. Give an example of one location, country, or state that would have the following climates:

   Tropical, rainy climate _____

   Tundra _____

   Subarctic _____ _____

   Desert _____

   Steppe _____

3. If you wanted to move to a densely populated city, where would you move?

   _____

   In what country is this city located? _____

   What type of climate would you expect in January? _____

   What is the annual amount of rainfall for this city? _____

   What type of vegetation might you find here? _____

4. If you were flying directly from Brisbane, Australia to Rome, Italy, approximately how many miles would you have traveled?

   _____

   Would this be closer or farther than to fly directly from New York to Rome?

   _____

   What is the difference? _____

5. Compare the square miles of Switzerland and Sweden. Which country's area is the largest? _____

   By how many square miles? _____

   Compare the population per square mile. What did you find out?

   _____

6. In what large city would you be if you were in eastern Argentina at the 35° South latitude?

   _____

   What is the average annual rainfall for this city? _____

   What type of climate would you find there? _____

Name _____  Date _____

Reference Book
Review Sheet

Directions: Use the reference books which you have studied to answer the following questions. After answering each, include the name of the reference book and the page number where your answer was found. (Hint: Let the name of the reference book help you remember what it contains. Also, look for key words in the questions which might help you decide which reference book to use).

1. What is Nathan Hale famous for saying just before his execution? _____

   _____

   Reference Book _____ Page _____

2. When was the first school in America established? _____

   Reference Book _____ Page _____

3. Rod McKuen is a famous poet and singer. Find five interesting facts about him and list them.

   _____

   _____

   _____

   _____

   _____

   Reference Book _____ Page _____

4. Who holds the world's record for voluntarily staying awake?

   _____

   What is the record for this? _____

   Reference Book _____ Page _____

5. Find one quotation that you like about the subject ''fear.'' Copy the quotation and give its author.

   _____

   _____

   _____

   Reference Book _____ Page _____

6. If you were interested in a career in air transportation, what are at least four related careers you might choose?

   _____

   _____

   _____

   Reference Book _____ Page _____

Reference Book
Review Sheet

Continued

7. What was the pseudonym (pen name) of William Sydney Porter? _____
   Name four stories that he wrote:

   _____

   _____

   _____

   _____

   Reference Book _____ Page _____

8. Find three synonyms for the word "grotesque."

   _____

   Reference Book _____ Page _____

9. Draw a small map of Europe to show where the tiny country of Luxembourg exists.

   Reference Book _____ Page _____

10. The first radio broadcast from an airplane was in what year? _____
    To what city was the broadcast sent? _____

    Reference Book _____ Page _____

11. For what movie was Meryl Streep chosen to win an Oscar? _____

    _____

    Reference Book _____ Page _____

12. List three of the most densely populated areas in the world.

    _____

    Reference Book _____ Page _____

Reference Book Review Sheet

Continued

13. Name three synonyms for the word "erudite."

_____

Reference Book _____ Page _____

14. What did Ogden Nash say concerning the subject of "money"? _____

_____

_____

Reference Book _____ Page _____

15. Who holds the record for being the tallest woman in the world? _____

_____ How tall is she?_____

Reference Book _____ Page _____

16. What does the word "sphygmomanometer" mean? _____

_____

_____

Reference Book _____ Page _____

17. If you wanted to become a banker, what type of educational preparation is recommended?

_____

_____

Reference Book _____ Page _____

18. What was the lowest temperature (Fahrenheit) ever recorded in the state of Tennessee?

_____ What was the highest temperature (Fahrenheit) ever recorded in

that state?_____

Reference Book _____ Page _____

Chapter
II

Readers'
Guide
to
Periodical
Literature

Name _____ Date _____

Readers' Guide
to Periodical Literature

Study Guide

Directions: Using the *Readers' Guide to Periodical Literature*, complete the following:

1. Name of reference book _____

2. Fill in the following information:

   Author / Editor _____

   Publisher _____

   Place of Publication_____

   Date of Publication _____

3. What is a periodical?_____

4. In the *Readers' Guide*, how are entries entered?

   _____

   _____

5. Abbreviations are used for names of periodicals. Where would you look to find the name of the magazine abbreviated?

   _____

   _____

6. Compare a subject entry with an author entry for the same article. (Hint: Look up a subject and choose an article. Find out its author and look up the article under the author's name.)

   How are the two entries similar and how are they different?_____

   _____

   _____

7. When looking up an article on a certain subject, you may come across the words ''see also.''

   What does this mean? _____

   _____

   What is the difference between ''see also'' and ''see''? _____

   _____

Name _____  Date _____

Readers' Guide
to Periodical Literature

Activity Sheet

Directions: Use the *Readers' Guide to Periodical Literature* to complete the following:

1. The *Readers' Guide* indexes approximately 125 periodicals. Of those indexed, to which ten would you prefer to subscribe?

   _____

   _____

   _____

   _____

   _____

   _____

   _____

   _____

   _____

   _____

   _____

2. List the subheads found in the *Readers' Guide* for each of the following subjects:
   A. Sports_____

   _____

   B. Television _____

   _____

   C. Crime _____

   _____

3. What do the following abbreviations in *Readers' Guide* represent? Explain those with an asterisk before it (*).
   A. Je _____
   B. D _____
   *C. bi-M _____
   D. pub_____

Directions: Using the *Readers' Guide to Periodical Literature*, complete the following:

   *E. jt auth_____
   F. Ap _____

▼

Readers' Guide
to Periodical Literature

Activity Sheet Continued

*G. q _____

*H. cond _____

4. Which magazine do the following abbreviations represent:

A. Sat Eve Post _____

B. Sci Am _____

C. Bsns W _____

D. N Y Times Mag _____

5. Under which headings would you look to find information on the movie *Star Wars*?

_____

A. Locate two articles on the subject of *Star Wars*. List the author's name, title of article, name of magazine, date of publication, volume number, and page numbers for each of the articles you selected.

_____

_____

B. Of the articles listed above, which do you think would give the best information to you if you were writing a critique of the movie, *Star Wars*?

_____

Explain your answer. _____

_____

6. If you were asked to do a research paper on the subject of unemployment in the United States, what subheadings would you divide this broad subject into?

_____

_____

Select one of the subheadings you chose and identify two articles you would use to help you write your paper. Remember to include the necessary information about each article.

_____

_____

_____

Readers' Guide Review Sheet

Directions: Using the *Readers' Guide to Periodical Literature*, identify the three **best** articles you might read to get information for each of the subjects listed below. For each article, list all the information you would need in order to not only find the article, but to complete a bibliography. For each article be sure to include the following: Author, Title of Article, Name of Magazine, Date of Publication, Volume Number, and Page Numbers.

1. Mardi Gras _____
_____
_____
_____
_____

2. The Statue of Liberty _____
_____
_____
_____
_____

3. Seminole Indians _____
_____
_____
_____
_____

4. Sharks _____
_____
_____
_____
_____

5. Photography _____
_____
_____
_____
_____

Chapter III

Encyclopedias

Name _____  Date _____

Encyclopedia

Study Guide

Directions: Using the most appropriate encyclopedia, complete the following:

1. Name of reference book _____

2. Publisher _____
   Place of publication _____
   Date of publication _____

3. What is provided to keep information in the encyclopedia updated?
   _____

4. Are guide words provided? _____ If so, what value are they? _____
   _____

5. If you are looking up a specific topic, how would the index be helpful?
   _____

   Is the index the only way you can locate information on a topic? _____
   Explain. _____
   _____

   Where is the index located (i.e. separate volume, end of individual volume, etc.)?
   _____

6. What type of visual aids are provided (i.e. graphs, tables, illustrations, etc.)?
   _____
   _____

7. What information do cross references provide? _____
   _____

8. What type of information does this encyclopedia provide?
   _____
   _____

Name _____   Date _____

Encyclopedia

Study Guide Continued

9. Many encyclopedia articles are lengthy, thus they are divided into main headings and subheadings. This division helps to make the investigation of the topic simpler. For example, if you were to research astronaut you might find the following:

Selection of Astronauts (main heading)

Requirements (subheading)

Screening (subheading)

Training the Astronaut (main heading)

Classroom Training (subheading)

Survival Training (subheading)

Research *Assyria* and give the main headings and subheadings.

_____
_____
_____
_____

What Did You Uncover?

Directions: Upon completion of the activity sheet(s) assigned, answer the following:

1. When researching a specific topic, why would you use an encyclopedia rather than a book on that topic?

_____

2. What was most helpful to you in the encyclopedia in regard to locating the information you needed?

_____

3. If you needed to do further research on a particular topic, how can the encyclopedia lead you to additional information?

_____
_____

Where in the World Am I?

Activity Sheet

Directions: Use the appropriate encyclopedia(s) and complete the following:

1. Often times and places have become immortalized in books. Describe the settings (time and place) for each of the following novels:

   The Adventures of Tom Sawyer by Mark Twain _____

   _____

   War and Peace by Tolstoy_____

   _____

   A Tale of Two Cities by Charles Dickens _____

   _____

   If you could be a character in one of these books, which would you choose?

   _____

   Why? _____

   _____

2. Names such as Jesse James, Billy the Kid, Wyatt Earp, and Wild Bill Hickok were associated with the excitement of the Western Frontier. Explain why each man is remembered today.

   Jesse James _____

   _____

   Billy the Kid_____

   _____

   Wyatt Earp _____

   _____

   Wild Bill Hickok _____

   _____

   Which of these would you consider a hero?_____

   Defend your answer. _____

   _____

   _____

   _____

From *Unlocking the Secrets of Research*, Copyright © 1986 Scott, Foresman and Company

Where in the World Am I?

Activity Sheet Continued

3. What do the Mojave, Painted and Gobi have in common?

_____

List characteristics that places such as these have in common. _____

_____

Describe how a person could best survive in such a place.

_____

4. Where in the world would you be if you were to visit the following site? Next to each, explain why it is such a significant area.

Little Big Horn_____

_____

Yorktown _____

_____

Hiroshima_____

_____

Which scene can you least justify? _____

Explain your answer. _____

5. *Casablanca* was the title of a famous movie. It is also the name of a famous city. Where is Casablanca?

_____

From what you have read about the city and the people who live there, write a **descriptive** account of "Life in Casablanca."

_____

_____

_____

_____

_____

_____

_____

Piñatas, Fireworks and Totem Poles

Activity Sheet

Directions: Using the most appropriate encylcopedia(s), complete the following:

1. What things might you find carved on a totem pole? _____

   _____

   What different purposes do totem poles serve?

   _____

   Design a totem pole for your family. Explain the different objects you selected for it.

   _____

   _____

   _____

   _____

   _____

   _____

   _____

   _____

2. What is another name for fireworks? _____

   For what holiday celebration in the United States are fireworks used?

   _____

   In what ways can fireworks be used, other than for celebrating?

   _____

   Think of a use for fireworks, not mentioned in your reference book, that may be helpful.

   _____

3. Name five games that were played by children in the early 1700s and are still being played today.

   _____

   _____

   Choose one of the games you have listed and compare how it is played in the U.S. with the way it is played in another country.

   _____

   _____

   _____

▼

From *Unlocking the Secrets of Research*, Copyright © 1986 Scott, Foresman and Company

Piñatas, Fireworks and Totem Poles

Activity Sheet Continued

4. Where did the following customs associated with marriage originate?

   a. giving an engagement ring _____

   b. wearing a veil _____

   _____

   c. carrying bride over threshold _____

5. Dancing is one of the oldest art forms and customs. Where can the earliest records of dancing be found? _____

   What are some reasons why primitive people danced? _____

   _____

   Which country is each of the following dances associated with and for what occasion was it used?

Dance	Country	Occasion
Bugaku dance		
Split-feather dance		
Nautch dance		
Hoop dance		
Pyrrhic dance		

6. From the myths written we can get insights into particular cultures. Why did people write myths?

   _____

   How did the people of ancient Greece view their gods?

   _____

   How is a myth different from a legend? _____

   _____

   _____

   Locate the origin of the following symbols:

   The serpent and the staff _____

   _____

   Cupid and arrow _____

What Makes It Tick?

Activity Sheet

Directions: Using the most appropriate encyclopedia(s), complete the following:

1. Most of us have wished at one time or another that we had a machine to do this or that for us. For example, we may say, ``If only there was a machine that could clean my room for me. . .'' Think of a gadget or a machine that has not been invented that you would like to have. Describe and illustrate what this machine might be like.

   _____

   _____

   _____

   _____

   Why do you think ``your machine'' has never been invented?

   _____

   What would you call your machine? _____

   If you invented something you would want to get a patent. Why?

   _____

   Who was the first person in the U.S. to get a patent? _____

   What did he invent? _____

2. Where did the word magnet come from? _____

   According to legend, how was magnetism discovered?_____

   _____

   What is the name of the rock that attracts magnets? _____

   What are some important uses of the magnet? _____

   _____

3. If you were in a submarine that was submerged under water and you wanted to see above the surface of the water, what instrument would be necessary? _____

   _____ Describe how this instrument works. _____

   _____

What Makes It Tick?

Activity Sheet Continued

What are some other uses for this instrument? _____

_____

4. What compound is put into the head of a match that makes it light? _____

What else is the match head made of? _____

What is the matchstick coated with? _____ Why? _____

Who made the first match that could be ignited by friction?

_____

What year? _____ The following types of matches were used prior to the invention of a friction light match. Briefly describe each.

Roman match or spunk_____

_____

Instantaneous light box _____

_____

5. Who invented the telescope? _____

What was his occupation? _____

In what year did he invent the telescope? _____ How is it believed the telescope was invented? _____

Who was the man who improved on the first telescope and used it for looking out to sea as well as into the sky?

_____

For what else was this person well known?

_____

_____

6. What is the difference between a refracting telescope and a reflecting telescope?

_____

Where is the world's largest refracting telescope located? _____

What is the size of the largest lens in this telescope?_____

What is the largest reflecting telescope and where is it located?

_____

Somewhere
Over the Rainbow
Activity Sheet

Directions: Use the appropriate encylcopedia(s) and complete the following:

1. What is another name for the Devil's Triangle? _____
   What areas are included within the triangle?

   _____

   What strange happenings have occured within that area?

   _____

   Which of the two names for this area do you think is most appropriate?

   _____

   Why? _____

   _____

   Create your own name for the triangle. _____
2. Describe a solar eclipse. _____

   _____

   Describe a lunar eclipse. _____

   _____

   Which of these are potentially harmful? _____
   Why? _____
3. What is a constellation? _____

   _____

   Select a constellation in our galaxy. _____
   From where did it get its name?

   _____

   On the back of this page, at the top, draw the constellation and include its main or important stars. On the bottom, include the same stars, in their same position, but connect them in a different way. Give your new constellation an appropriate name.

4. Where does space begin? _____

   _____

   What is the biggest problem to overcome in order to enter space?

   _____

   To survive space, what factors must be considered?

   _____

From *Unlocking the Secrets of Research*, Copyright © 1986 Scott, Foresman and Company

Somewhere Over the Rainbow

Activity Sheet Continued

5. We now know that the Earth revolves around the sun. Long ago, however, man believed the sun moved and attempted to explain its movements. Research myths relating to the movement of the sun. Summarize one of these.

_____

_____

_____

_____

_____

6. Astronauts and cosmonauts have had the opportunity to explore "Somewhere Over the Rainbow." Read about their various space missions and list the **three** whom you consider to be the most important "Space Pioneers." Defend your answer.

_____

_____

_____

_____

_____

_____

7. When did man first walk on the moon?_____

Who is credited with this feat? _____

What were the first words spoken as he stepped on the moon?

_____

If you were the first person to walk on the moon, what historic words would you utter?

_____

_____

_____

_____

_____

Name _____ Date _____

All Animals
Great and Small

Activity Sheet

Directions: Use the appropriate encylcopedia(s) and complete the following:

1. Poodles, Siamese cats, mules, and many other animals were not in existence during cavemen and/or prehistoric times. Why not?

   _____

   How did these, as well as many other animals, come into existence?

   _____

   If you could create a new animal, what would it be like? Describe and draw a picture in the box to illustrate it.

   _____

   _____

   _____

   _____

   _____

   _____

   What would you name this animal? _____

2. Animals are found throughout the world; however, some animals are associated with a particular continent. For example, you would not find an elephant roaming through North America or a polar bear in South America. List two animals that are indigenous to each of the following continents:

   North America   _____   _____

   South America   _____   _____

   Africa   _____   _____

   Europe   _____   _____

   Asia   _____   _____

   Antarctica   _____   _____

   Australia   _____   _____

   Why is it true that you only find certain animals in certain places? _____

   _____

3. Many animals live in their mothers' pouches. Name three animals that live in pouches.

   _____

   In what country are most pouched animals found?_____

80

All Animals
Great and Small

Activity Sheet Continued

What one pouched animal is found in North America? _____

Why is it necessary for these animals to live in a pouch? _____

_____

What is another name for animals that carry their young in pouches? _____

4. Many of the animals that are tame (domesticated) today were at one time wild. What was the first animal to be tamed? _____

How do you think the taming of this animal came about?

_____

What other animals were once wild that are now tame?

_____

5. What are four different kinds of apes?

_____

Of these four apes, which is the largest and most powerful? _____

The most intelligent? _____ The one that looks most like man? _____

_____ The one that walks erect and has very long arms? _____

How are apes different from monkeys? _____

_____

6. For each of the following animals or animal groups, give the literal or exact meaning of the name.

Aardvark _____

Amphibian _____

Albino _____

Reptile _____

Rhinoceros _____

Choose one of these animals and tell why you think the name is appropriate.

_____

_____

Name _____ Date _____

Encyclopedia Review Sheet

Directions: Answer the following questions by using one of the encyclopedias in your school library or classroom. List the **name of the encyclopedia** used, the **volume**, and the **page number**. Be sure to use a variety of sources.

1. How was Pompeii destroyed? _____
_____

    Encyclopedia _____ Volume _____ Page _____

2. List five different topics your encyclopedia lists under the subject of "astronomy."
_____
_____

    Encyclopedia _____ Volume _____ Page _____

3. Through which states does the Mississippi River flow? _____
_____

    Encyclopedia _____ Volume _____ Page _____

    By what name is it affectionately known? _____

    Encyclopedia _____ Volume _____ Page _____

4. According to mythology, who is Ares? _____

    By what other name is he known? _____

    Encyclopedia _____ Volume _____ Page _____

5. Name three types of poisonous snakes and tell where they are found.
_____
_____

    Encyclopedia _____ Volume _____ Page _____

6. Comparing the different encyclopedias you have available to you, answer the following:

    Which set is the most comprehensive in terms of information provided?
_____

    Which set is best organized in terms of making it easier for the researcher to locate specific information? _____

7. In what volumes of an encyclopedia other than volume "V" can you find information on Valentine's Day?
_____

8. Why is it important when researching a topic to use more than one set of encyclopedias?
_____

Chapter
IV

Writing A Bibliography, Footnotes, and Endnotes

Bibliography

Study Guide

Directions: Read and become familiar with the following information.

What is a bibliography?

A bibliography is a list of books, magazines, and other sources from which you get information on a certain topic. It is arranged alphabetically, according to the first word, whether it is the author's name, editor's name, name of the book, or title of an article. All the lines in a bibliographic entry except the first one is indented three spaces. There are several accepted formats for writing a bibliography. The examples given below follow one of these.

What is the general format for a book reference?

author's name, last name first
title, underlined
book edition (if indicated)
place of publication
publisher's name in full
year of publication

What are the various ways to list standard books in a bibliography?

1. No author listed (Example)

   A Manual of Style. 13th ed. (Chicago: University of Chicago Press,(1982)).

2. One author (Example)

   Lester, James. Writing Research Papers: A Complete Guide. 4th ed. Glenview, Ill.: Scott, Foresman and Company, 1984.

3. Two authors (Example)

   Corder, Jim W., and Ruszkiewicz, John J. Handbook of Current English. 7th ed. Glenview, Ill.: Scott, Foresman and Company, 1985.

4. Three authors (Example)

   Berelson, Bernard R.; Lazarsfeld, Paul F.; and McPhee, William. Voting. Chicago: University of Chicago Press, 1954.

5. Edited Work (Example)

   Steward, Joyce S., ed. Contemporary College Reader. 3rd ed. Glenview, Ill.: Scott, Foresman and Company, 1985.

Bibliography

Study Guide Continued

What is the general format for a periodical (magazine) reference?

author's name, last name first
title of article, in quotation marks
name of magazine, underlined
date of publication
page reference

How is a magazine listed?

1. An article from a monthly magazine (Example)

    Eliot, John L. "Isle Royale." <u>National Geographic</u>, April 1985, pp. 534-550.

How are articles in reference works (*Encyclopedias, Who's Who, Current Biographies*, etc.) listed?

1. Author known (Example)

    <u>The World Book Encyclopedia</u>, 1985 ed. S.v. "Airplane," by Martin Caidin.

2. Author unknown (Example)

    <u>The World Book Encyclopedia</u>, 1985 ed. S.v. "Antarctic Ocean."

Note: the abbreviation "S.v." in the references above indicates the subject under which you should look.

Bibliography

Activity Sheet

Directions: Complete the following:

1. If you were asked to create a two line "blurb" on the function of a bibliography, what would you include?

   _____

   _____

2. Bibliographies are usually located in one of two different places in a book. Look through various books and find out where these two places are.

   _____

   _____

3. In some bibliographies you will find the following abbreviations. What do they mean?

   et al. _____

   pp. _____

   vol. _____

   ed. _____

4. Organize the following information into correct bibliographic form for a book: 1960 Little Women Scholastic Book Services Louisa May Alcott New York. Organize the following information into correct bibliography form for an encyclopedia article: ed. 1962 The World Book Encyclopedia Painting

   _____

   _____

   _____

5. Select three books on the subject of Helen Keller. Write a bibliography for the books (list them in alphabetical order).

   _____

   _____

   _____

   _____

   _____

   _____

Bibliography

Activity Sheet Continued

6. Locate two encyclopedia articles on the subject of dreams. Write a bibliography to include them (list them according to the order in which they would appear in a bibliography).

_____

_____

_____

_____

_____

7. Select two articles from a magazine(s). Write a bibliography for these articles (list them in alphabetical order).

_____

_____

_____

_____

_____

8. When gathering information on a reference book for a bibliography, what information should you make sure you record?

_____

_____

9. Tell three different reasons why a reader would find a bibliography useful.

_____

_____

_____

Footnotes/Endnotes

Study Guide

Directions: Read and become familiar with the following information.

What are footnotes and endnotes?

Footnotes are notes of explanation or references found at the bottom of the page. Endnotes are references collected at the end of the paper, chapter, or book. Both footnotes and endnotes tell where you can find the source of the information given in the body of the text.

Footnotes and endnotes are indicated in the body of the text by a number which corresponds to the number found in one of the three places where they are recorded. Notes are numbered consecutively (1,2,3, . . .). These numbers should be written or typed slightly above the line. They are place right after the final punctuation marks in the material being quoted or referred to.

How are quotes referenced?

1. Note in text (Example)

   Meinbach and Rothlein state that "traditionally, students have consulted general encyclopedias for any information they might need."[1]

2. Referencing the quote in a footnote or endnote (Example)

   [1]Anita Meinbach and Liz Rothlein, <u>Unlocking the Secrets of Research</u> (Glenview, Ill.: Scott, Foresman and Company, 1986). p. 1.

What is the general format for a footnote/endnote in a book reference?

author's name, as it appears on the title page
title, underlined
edition (if indicated)
place of publication
publisher's name in full
year of publication
page reference

The first line in a footnote/endnote entry is indented. There are several accepted formats for writing footnotes/endnotes.The examples given below follow one of these.

What are the various ways to list books?

1. No author listed (Example)

   <u>A Manual of Style</u>, 13th ed. (Chicago: University of Chicago Press, (1982)), pp. 135-37.

2. One author (Example)

   James Lester, <u>Writing Research Papers: A Complete Guide</u>, 4th ed. (Glenview, Ill.: Scott, Foresman and Company, 1984), pp. 103-5.

Footnotes/Endnotes

Study Guide Continued

3. Two authors (Example)

   Jim W. Corder and John J. Ruszkiewicz, <u>Handbook of Current English</u>, 7th ed. (Glenview, Ill.: Scott, Foresman and Company, 1985), p 50.

4. Three authors (Example)

   Bernard R. Berelson, Paul F. Lazarsfeld, and William McPhee, <u>Voting</u> (Chicago: University of Chicago Press, 1954), pp. 93-95.

5. Edited work (Example)

   Joyce S. Steward, ed., <u>Contemporary College Reader</u>, 3rd ed. (Glenview, Ill: Scott, Foresman and Company, 1985), pp. 3-5.

What is the general format for a footnote/endnote in a periodical reference?

author's name, as it appears on the title page
title of article, in quotation marks
name of magazine, underlined
date of publication
page reference

How is a magazine listed?

1. An article from a monthly magazine (Example)

   John L. Eliot, "Isle Royale," <u>National Geographic</u>, April 1985, p. 536.

How are articles in referenced works (*Encyclopedias, Who's Who, Current Biographies,* etc.) listed?

1. Author known (Example)

   The <u>World Book Encyclopedia</u>, 1985 ed., s.v. "Airplane," by Martin Caidin.

2. Author unknown (Example)

   The <u>World Book Encyclopedia</u>, 1985 ed., s.v. "Antarctic Ocean."

Note: the abbreviation "s.v." in the references above indicates the subject under which you should look.

Name _____  Date _____

Footnotes/Endnotes

Activity Sheet

Directions: Complete the following:

1. If you are involved in writing a research paper, why is it important to include footnotes/endnotes?

    _____

2. How can footnotes/endnotes be of benefit to a person who is reading a selection that contains these notes?

    _____

3. In many footnotes/endnotes you will find the abbreviation "ibid." What does the term mean?

    _____

4. Footnotes/endnotes can be located in one of three different places in a book. Look through various textbooks and find the location of at least two of these places.

    _____

5. Organize the following information into correct footnote/endnote for a book: Lancer Books Inc. Robert Louis Stevenson p. 4 New York 1957 Kidnapped. Organize the following information into correct footnote/endnote form for a periodical: 76-89 The Next Frontier? National Geographic 150.1 Issac Asimov July 1976

    _____

    _____

    _____

6. When is it necessary to use footnotes/endnotes?

    _____

7. Imagine that you have quoted several lines from an encyclopedia article on the subject of "motion pictures." Select an article that you may have used for this purpose and write a footnote for it.

    _____

    _____

8. If you were doing a research paper and wanted to quote a statistic about the number of people who live in New York City, how would you write the footnote?

    _____

    _____

    _____

Chapter V

Applying Your Research Skills

Focusing Topics

Activity Sheet

Often when you select a topic for a research paper you may tend to choose a topic that is too broad. When this happens it is impossible to do an in-depth coverage of your topic. Therefore, ''don't bite off more than you can chew.'' Narrow your topic into something manageable.

For example, if you were to choose the subject ''astronomy'' it would be too broad because volumes and volumes have been written on this topic. You would need to focus on what aspect of astronomy you wished to research, for example: planets, stars, galaxies, constellations, meteors, or people who have made discoveries in astronomy.

Directions: If you were given the following subjects, what would be the possible topics on which you could focus?

Subject   Focused Topics

1. Magic
   _____
   _____
   _____
   _____
   _____

2. Computers
   _____
   _____
   _____
   _____
   _____

3. Mark Twain
   _____
   _____
   _____
   _____
   _____

Name _____  Date _____

Selecting Reference Books
Activity Sheet

You have had the opportunity to investigate a variety of reference books. You should now know how each is organized and what types of information each includes. You are now ready to use your skills in selecting the appropriate book(s) for gathering information. Remember, your research can be as exciting an experience as you allow it to be. The more variety of reference books you use, the more rewarding it becomes.

Directions: If you were given the following subjects, what would be one possible topic on which you could focus? List reference books which you could consult for information.

Subject	Focused Topic	Reference Books
1. New York City	_____	_____
		_____
		_____
		_____
2. Weather phenomenon	_____	_____
		_____
		_____
		_____
3. Barbara Streisand	_____	_____
		_____
		_____
		_____
4. Motion Pictures	_____	_____
		_____
		_____
		_____

Organizing and Outlining Research Topics

Activity Sheet

Outlining

After you have focused the topic, it will be necessary to prepare an outline. Outlining will help you to organize your thoughts and help you see how the various information gathered fits together to create your paper. The following is a suggested format for outlining:

Title
I. Main Topic
  A. Important Subtopic
    1. Minor Subtopic
    2. Minor Subtopic
  B. Important Subtopic
  C. Important Subtopic
    1. Minor Subtopic
    2. Minor Subtopic
      a. Detail
      b. Detail

Overweight
I. Causes of overweight
  A. Slow metabolism
  B. Lack of exercise
  C. Poor eating habits
    1. Over eating
    2. Poor nutrition
II. Results of overweight
  A. Medical problems
    1. High blood pressure
    2. Increased risk of heart attack
  B. Lethargic
  C. Poor self-concept
    1. Appearance
    2. Other perceptions

Directions: Choose one of the following broad subjects, focus it, and prepare an outline below:

Reptiles, Marathon Running, Theatres, or World War II.

Organizing and Outlining Research Topics

Taking Notes

Once you have prepared your outline, you are ready to begin your research. As you collect information for your research paper it is necessary for you to take notes. To make your note taking more efficient and beneficial, the following suggestions are offered:

1. For each reference book selected, prepare a separate note card or paper.
2. On this note card, record pertinent information — DON'T COPY everything word for word, except direct quotes. These quotes must be exact and indicated in quotation marks.
3. For each reference book used, be sure to include on the note card all bibliographical information.

Now that you have all your notes, you may ask ''What's next?''

1. Revise your outline, if necessary, to reflect additional ideas and information gathered from research.
2. Begin to write a rough draft of your paper pulling ideas from your note cards as you follow your outline.
3. When you use direct quotations, statistics, or information that needs documentation, be sure to indicate with a footnote/endnote number. On a separate piece of paper, write down the corresponding footnote/endnote number and its reference.
4. Edit and proof read your rough draft.
5. Before preparing the final copy, decide if you are using endnotes or footnotes.
6. Type or write (in ink) your final copy of the paper.
7. Prepare your bibliography to reflect all reference materials used.

Directions: Choose a subject of your choice (including any suggested in this chapter). Follow these steps and prepare your reserch paper:

1. Focus your topic
2. Select possible reference books
3. Outline
4. Take notes on each reference
5. Revise outline
6. Write rough draft
7. Edit and proof read
8. Prepare final copy

Annotated Bibliography of Reference Books

The following books were used in preparing the worksheet questions contained in Unlocking the Secrets of Research. If you are unable to obtain any of these books, you can easily substitute other reference material. The substitutions of other similar reference books will not effect the objectives of this book.

Bartlett's Book of Familiar Quotations
A collection of passages, phrases and proverbs. There is both an author index and a subject index.

Current Biography Yearbook
Brief information about living leaders in all fields. This is arranged alphabetically. (Note: the people included in the book were alive at the time the book was published.)

Dictionary
There are many types of dictionaries. They include the words used in our language, their meanings, correct pronunciations, syllabication, accents, parts of speech, origin, etc. The dictionary also includes other varied information such as abbreviations, origins of words, a table of measurements, and a **brief** mention of people and places.

Encyclopedia
A comprehensive reference work that contains information on a wide range of subjects or on numerous aspects of a particular field.

Encyclopedia of Careers and Vocational Guidance
A book designed to aid in early career planning. It provides a variety of information on a wide spectrum of careers.

Famous First Facts
A record of first happenings, discoveries and inventions in the U.S. The material is arranged alphabetically, by subject.

Guinness Book of World Records
Gives names, places and dates of various accomplishments that have been world records.

Readers' Guide to Periodical Literature
An extremely valuable book for use in research which lists, by subject, all the different magazine articles that deal with the subject. Articles can be located by author name as well. *Readers' Guide* gives the name, volume, date of publication, and page on which the information can be found.

Thesaurus
Contains numerous synonyms for words and also gives antonyms.

Twentieth Century Authors
A biographical dictionary that briefly describes the lives of writers of this century from all nations of the world whose words are read in English. It is arranged alphabetically, and the major works of these authors are also included.

Webster's Biographical Dictionary
Brief information about famous people of all nationalities, living and dead.

Who's Who in America
Contains brief information about famous Americans only. This book contains only those people who were living at the time of publication.

World Almanac
Contains all types of statistical information including a yearly calendar of days, weeks, and months, with astronomical data, weather forecasts and a variety of tables. There is a detailed index which tells where things in the book can be found.

World Atlas
Contains geographical and statistical information in the form of maps and pictures.

Answer Key

Note:
Depending on the source and volume used, answers may vary. The sources from which answers were obtained are listed in the "Study Guide," (answers one and two).

Chapter I

Familiar Quotations
Study Guide

1. *Familiar Quotations*

2. Bartlett, John; Little Brown and Company; Toronto; 1982.

3. short for ibidemi, "in the same place"; means that the source of a quotation is the same as the preceding cited source.

4. will vary, however, the answer should include: authors and quotations for which they are credited as well as a source or identification line which helps the reader locate the work from which the quotation is taken.

5. The main index is located at the back of the book. This index contains phrases arranged alphabetically by a key word. After each phrase the page number and quote number in which the phrase appears is given. In addition, an "Index of Authors" at the front of the book supplies birth and death date of each author and the page numbers on which their quotes can be found.

6. The number of the quotation on the page.

Activity Sheet A

1. "Learning without thought is labor lost, thought without learning is perilous."

2. answers will vary

3. "And so, my fellow Americans, ask not what your country can do for you; ask what you can do for your country."

4. "All the lonely people, where do they all belong?"; "Eleanor Rigby"

5. "Play it again Sam;" 1969

6. Anna Eleanor Roosevelt; answers will vary

7. In his own words, Muhammed Ali said, "I am the greatest."; Cassius Clay

8. *Frankenstein*

Activity Sheet B

1. Benjamin Franklin; *Poor Richard's Almanac*

2. "The world would go round a deal faster than it does."

3. answers will vary

4. *King Lear*; answers will vary depending upon interpretation; answers will vary

5. stale; eternity; answers will vary depending upon interpretation

6. "The gods help them that help themselves."; answers will vary

Current Biography Yearbook
Study Guide

1. *Current Biography Yearbook*

2. Charles Moritz; H.W. Wilson, Co.; N.Y.; 1983

3. it provides the student, reference librarian, or any other researcher with brief, objective, accurate, and well-documented biographical articles about living leaders in all fields of accomplishment the world over

4. every year

5. by looking in the index and then looking through the appropriate year book alphabetically; look in the *Current Bio-*

graphy *Cumulative Index 1940-1970;* look in the index of the 1980 yearbook

6. to provide additional books and periodicals where the reader can go to find out more information about the person; portrait

7. look in the rear volume for full name

8. pronunciation of the name if it is unusual, date of birth, occupation, and address

9. it tells the year of the yearbook where you would find the biography for that person; it indicates there is an obituary for that person in the yearbook for the year following the name; for persons whose biographies have been published in an earlier edition of *Current Biography Yearbook* and are now dead

10. in the heading it will say this article supercedes the article which appeared earlier in whatever *Current Biography Yearbook* it was in.

Activity Sheet A

1. his stunt and death-defying jumps on his motorcycle; "the last gladiator in the New Rome;" ski jumping, ice hockey, pole-vaulting; W. Clement Stone and Norman Vincent Peale

2. Look in the back of the book; you will find people classified by professions; answers will vary; answers will vary; answers will vary

3. answers may vary from *Saturday Night Live* to movies such as *48 Hours* and *Trading Places;* answers will vary depending on year Activity Sheet is done. He was born in 1961; he hosted a talent show at the Roosevelt Youth Center in N.Y.; Richard Pryor; answers will vary; answers will vary

4. as President of the U.S.; answers will vary depending on when Study Sheet in completed. Mr. Reagan was born in 1911; in a flat above a general store on Main Street, Tampico, Ill.; actor, Governor of California, congressman, sportscaster; Irish; answers will vary

5. Frank Shorter; a businessman; he heads

Bill Rogers and Co., a manufacturing firm for running togs; 18; Ambrose Burfoot; answers will vary

6. answers will vary

Activity Sheet B

1. answers may vary, however the similarities may be that they are both singers, they both live in N.Y., they both performed on Broadway; answers may vary; however, the differences may be Sills is a coloratiya soprana and sings operas whereas Holliday is a contralla and sings jazz, rock, and gospel; Holliday is younger than Sills; answers may vary; answers may vary but you might expect *Dreamgirls,* a Broadway musical; answers will vary;

2. a former movie star and Princess of Monaco; *The Country Girl;* Prince Rainier III; she met him at the Cannes Film Festival; three; she died in an automobile accident; 1983

3. Sally Ride was the first American woman to fly in space and Valentina Tereshkova was the first woman in the world to fly in space; 20 years; parachute jumping; athletics — baseball, football, and tennis; answers will vary

4. 1983, 1972; because he went from being a U.S. Permanent Representative to the United Nations to being Vice President of the United States; that his real name was Herbert Walker but he is known and goes by George Bush; answers will vary

5. answers may vary, however. they are both singers and both live in California; Kenny Rogers; 28 years; answers will vary

6. an educator or full professor, Dept. of Special Education at the University of Southern California; "Dr. Love" and the "hug therapist;" "I think if I had a single wish in all this world it would be to give **you** back to **you**;" answers will vary; took a sabbatical leave, traveled around the world, and studied a variety of cultures

The Dictionary
Study Guide

1. *Scott, Foresman Intermediate Dictionary*

2. a key which aids the user in the pronunciation of unfamiliar words. It gives examples of words using certain diacritical marks to help the user understand the sounds each mark represents; found at the beginning of the dictionary and in many dictionaries at the bottom of each page

3. The different meanings of a word are generally given in the order of their frequency of use — the most common meaning is put first while the least common is put last. There are, however, exceptions.

4. answers may vary but should contain the fact that an abridged version is a condensed one — not nearly as comprehensive as the unabridged. The unabridged dictionary attempts to record all literate pronunciations of a particular word while the abridged usually includes those considered most correct. The abridged does, however, preserve the same format as the unabridged; answers will vary; answers will vary

5. an informal word or expression

6. depends on the dictionary — some include etymologies or origins while others do not

7. enables the user to look up words with greater speed

8. answers will vary

Activity Sheet A

1. penicillin; lieutenant; rhinoceros; kaleidoscope

2. answers will vary

3. lien

4. fire officials and police officials

5. collects coins; collects stamps

6. mē dē e′vəl or měd ē′vəl or mə dē′vəl

7. answers will vary

8. illusion

Activity Sheet B

1. True statements - a,c,

2. answers will vary

3. source of annoyance; to have an oppressive or destructive effect

4. answers will vary

5. to state or infer; person who chooses to make use of what he/she considers to be the best ideas from various systems of thought

6. foolishly romantic, idealistic; from Don Quixote — the idealistic hero in the novel *Don Quixote*
plant or flower; from Narcissus — in Greek legend, a man who fell in love with his own reflection and was changed into a flower
to tease with something out of reach; from Tantalus — in Greek mythology, a son of Zeus who was punished by being placed in water up to his neck and just out reach of fruit

7. answers will vary

Encyclopedia Of Careers and Vocational Guidance
Study Guide

1. *Encyclopedia of Careers and Vocational Guidance*

2. Hopke, William, ed.; J.G. Ferguson Publishing Co.; Chicago, Illinois; 1981

3. answers will vary but should include the idea that it's giving aid in the selction of a job or career

4. designed to help students, their parents, teachers and counselors, by providing a reference book which includes: information about a wide variety of careers and how to make appropriate career decisions

5. guidance articles and articles which describe a field or family of occupations; articles on **specific** careers with detailed information on all aspects of each career

6. answers will vary but should include the use of the table of contents and indexes in **both** volumes as well as the bibliography in Volume I, and the ''Related Articles'' which are found at the end of each career field description in Volume I

7. lists and summarizes books in various fields that can be consulted for additional information; arranged alphabetically according to subject matter

8. lists all accredited colleges and universities in the U.S. and Canada, summarizes the scope of the institutions, its general size, levels of degrees granted, who operate it, and information on the student body

9. includes the title and number which can be used to request government publications on various careers

Activity Sheet A

1. answers will vary

2. ''Bookkeeping Workers,'' ''Buyers,'' ''Cashiers,'' ''Salesworkers: Retail,'' ''Salesworkers: Wholesale''

3. general manager, business manager, television sports writer and researcher, sports announcer, newspaper sports writer and columnist, publicity, sports statistician, sports photographer, sports official, etc.

4. answers may vary but should include data that interpreters may apply directly to firms, or organizations — it may be necessary to work at a less prestigious position and then move up to interpreter; there is a great need for **good** linguists but fewer work in the U.S. than in any other part of the world. It's estimated that the demand for good interpreters will increase. Interpreters may also find work as translaters.

5. must be able to operate calmly under pressure, must be able to make good sound decisions quickly, etc.

6. answers will vary

Activity Sheet B

1. answers will vary

2. answers will vary but should include the fact that there has been a tremendous increase in computer technology thereby increasing the number of workers in all aspects of the field; answers will vary; answers will vary

3. optometrists - six years of college including lab and class work in optometry, primarily concerned with examining eyes, performing services to improve vision and eye care.
opticians - recent trend toward formal training in the form of two year program, use the prescriptions of opthalmologists and optometrists to make, fit, and adjust glasses
opthalmologist - medical school graduates with special training in the medical and surgical care of eyes. They prescribe drugs, perform surgery, and prescribe lenses and exercises; answers will vary

4. answers will vary

5. answers will vary

6. answers will vary

7. answers will vary

Famous First Facts
Study Guide

1. *Famous First Facts*

2. Kane, Joseph; H.G. Wilson Co.; N.Y.; 1981

3. ''Index by Years'' — facts arranged chronologically by year. Under each year the facts are arranged alphabetically by the headings under which they appear in the main body.
''Index by Days of the Month'' — facts arranged by the day of the year beginning with January 1. Under each day the facts are arranged chronologically by year.
''Index to Personal Names'' — arranged alphabetically by last name, the individuals listed are associated in some way

with the event described. Words in bold print indicate under which heading information relating to the person can be found. ''Geographical Index'' — arranged alphabetically by state. Under each state the cities are arranged alphabetically. Facts associated with the individual city are noted. The words in bold type indicate under which heading the fact can be found.

4. alphabetically according to subject

5. answers will vary

6. answers will vary

7. answers will vary

Activity Sheet A

1. first woman aviator, first woman to fly solo across the Pacific Ocean, first woman to make a transatlantic solo flight, first woman to receive the National Geographic Society Special gold medal

2. Bicycle velocipedes or swift walkers

3. It was invented by George Washington Gale **Ferris**; 1892

4. A solid state computer; the solid state computer had 100 times the capacity and ten times the speed of ENIAC, but took approximately 1/6 of the space

5. Andrew Johnson; 35 to 19 against Johnson which was one vote short of the 2/3 needed to impeach him

6. Thomas A. Edison; the electric incadescent lamp

7. answers will vary

8. it had fewer octaves and no hammers.

Activity Sheet B

1. Dr. Ralph Johnson Bunche; Look it up under the entry entitled ''Nobel Prize'' or in the ''Index by Days'' under December 10, 1950, or under the ''Year Index'' under the year 1950 and then look for ''Nobel Prize.''

2. Yes; the ice cream cone is said to have originated at the Louisiana Purchase Exposition in St. Louis, MO., in 1904. A sales-

man there gave a young lady an ice cream sandwich and some flowers. Since she didn't have a vase, she took one layer of the sandwich, rolled it up and formed a vase. She rolled the second layer in the same way to hold the ice cream and the ice cream cone was born!

3. Columbus' discovery of America; answers will vary

4. answers will vary

5. answers will vary

Guinness Book Of World Records
Study Guide

1. *Guinness Book of World Records*

2. Norris McWhirter; Bantam Books, Inc.; N.Y.; 1984

3. answers may vary but may include: to provide world records on a variety of events, topics and subjects

4. from the Guinness Brewing Company in Ireland that in 1920 was the largest in the world. They found this book to provide a means of settling peaceful arguments about record performances.

5. answers may vary but may include: they publish records that improve upon previously published records or which are newly significant in having become the subject of widespread and, preferably, worldwide competition

6. answers will vary

7. answers may vary but may include: having a signed authentication by an independent, impartial adult witness of standing in the community; signed log books that include order of events, times and duration of activity, etc.; from local or national newspapers, radio, or TV coverage

8. index or table of contents

Activity Sheet A

1. man eating spaghetti; 8.4 sec.

2. 20th and 21st Olympic Games; Pope John Paul II's visit to Ireland, and the World Cup Final in Madrid; answers will vary

3. answers will vary

4. chocolates; $429; Le Leruns; Charbonel et Walker

5. Jan. 27, 1926; Nov. 2, 1936; about 100 sets; yes; a television station in Berlin, Germany made a low definition transmission from March 22, 1935, but the transmitter burnt out in Aug. 1935

Activity Sheet B

1. answers will vary; answers will vary

2. any records involving consumption of more than 2 liters (approximately 2 quarts) of beer or any at all involving spirits, records involving potentially dangerous categories such as eating live ants, raw eggs with shells, etc.; because they are unsafe; answers will vary

3. India; Ireland; 26.5 years; voting ages range from 15 years of age in Philippines to 25 years of age in Andorra

4. 87 million; Marie Osmond; more; Juliet and Her Nurse painted by Joseph Mallord William Turner

5. answers will vary

6. answers will vary; answers will vary; answers will vary

7. State of the Vatican City; 728; no, because there is nil birth rate

8. answers will vary; answers will vary

The Thesaurus
Study Guide

1. *In Other Words - A Junior Thesaurus*

2. Andrew Schiller and William A. Jenkens; Scott, Foresman and Co.; Glenview, Ill.; 1982

3. A book of words that lists synonyms and antonyms of its entry words

4. A synonym has almost the same meaning as the other word, but there is usually some shade of difference between them

5. In some types the entry words are arranged alphabetically, others have the words arranged according to a general idea and an index is necessary to locate the entry word needed.

Activity Sheet A

1. answers will vary

2. spoke, told, declared, stated, affirmed, mentioned, etc.

3. answers will vary

4. wrath, fury, irritation, rage, annoyance, etc.

5. answers will vary, but one possibility: annoyance, irritation, anger, fury, rage, wrath

6. answers will vary

7. poor, indigent, poverty-stricken, penniless, destitute, insolvent, etc.

8. answers will vary

Activity Sheet B

1. answers may vary but can include: right (adj.) - correct, precise, exact, accurate, true; right (noun) - privilege, claim, grant; right (noun) - propriety, what should be, fitness;

2. synonyms - loud, noisy, loud-mouthed, etc.; antonyms - silent, quiet, etc.

3. answers will vary

4. answers will vary

5. answers will vary

6. answers will vary

Twentieth Century Authors
Study Guide

1. *Twentieth Century Authors*

2. Kunitz, Stanley; H.W. Wilson and Co.; N.Y.; 1955

3. includes biographies of authors selected for their reputation and/or popularity. Authors must be of the 20th century whose books are familiar to readers of English.

4. the following are not included because they were not writers in the 20th century: Shakespeare, Twain, Cervantes, Whitman, and Poe

5. pronunciation of names, list of principle works, other biographical and critical sources which could be referred to for further information about the author, as well as a sketch of the person's life and career

6. both; a large number of authors wrote their own sketches (autobiographical) and the balance was written by a person other than the author (biographical)

Activity Sheet A

1. Tarzan; Mars

2. answers will vary; answers will vary; mystery books; answers will vary

3. from city in which he was born, and from his family; awarded 1921 Pulitzer Prize for *Arrowsmith* and the 1930 Nobel Prize (to name two of the most important); answers will vary

4. bobbin-boy in a mill, teacher, cobbler, editor, and farmer; Wordsworth; in wisdom; answers will vary

5. from what he reads in the newspapers; answers will vary; answers will vary; a Memorial Hospital in N.Y., Will Rogers Library in Oklahoma, a tower erected by an admirer, to name a few

6. papered a wall in his room; answers will vary

7. Dr. Seuss; from his mother's maiden name and from the degree he always wanted but never earned; answers will vary

8. answers will vary

Activity Sheet B

1. pen name; O'Henry; answers will vary

2. he was born in India, learned of India's customs from those who helped raise him and lived in India for a time; answers will vary

3. Abraham Lincoln; the terms of the Pulitzer Prize prohibits giving the biography prize to works about Washington or Lincoln; answers will vary

4. Frederic Dannay and Manfred B. Lee; detective; answers will vary; answers will vary

5. he was a hobo and peddler by choice and later became a well-known writer; *Autobiography of a Super-Tramp*; answers will vary

6. answers will vary

7. answers will vary

Webster's Biographical Dictionary Study Guide

1. *Webster's Biographical Dictionary*

2. Neilson, W.A.; G. and C. Merriam Co.; Massachusetts; 1980

3. answers will vary, although they may include the fact that it is organized alphabetically as is a dictionary. It also contains the pronunciation of entries, a pronunciation key and syllabication, as well as an explanation of the entry.

4. answers will vary, although they may include the fact that the dictionary's main function is the definition of common words, while *Webster's Biographical Dictionary* includes the name and biographical sketches of famous people

5. colloquial, colloquially — informal words; anonymous, anonymously — unknown; obsolete — no longer used

6. answers will vary

7. entries represent a selection of names that were either inadvertently omitted from the main body or those whose inclusion became evident after the main body was printed. A few names in the addenda also appear on the main body but the addenda includes additional information.

Activity Sheet A

1. both are involved in the field of music; the writing of operas - *Hansel and Gretel* and *Die Königskinder*; Humperdinck composed music for some of Shakespeare's plays

2. Socrates; accused of impiety and corrupting youth; Plato's writings reflect the philosophy of Socrates who didn't leave any written records

3. John Jay, John Rutledge, Oliver Elisworth; the U.S. Senate didn't confirm him

4. animals and the American West; cowboy and correspondent during the Spanish-American War

5. K'ung Futzo (or Kung Futse or K'ung Ch'iu) — literally means Philosopher Kung; brief record of his teachings

Activity Sheet B

1. the American struggle for Independence; he encourage the English people to overthrow their monarchy and organize a republic; answers will vary

2. George and Charles Merriam purchased the publication rights to Webster's *An American Dictionary of the English Language* from Noah Webster's heirs; 1847

3. in 1900 as the result of the generosity of Helen Miller Gould Shepard; answers will vary; answers will vary; answers will vary; answers will vary

4. *History of the Expedition Under the Commands of Captains Lewis and Clark;* Lewis and Clark

5. Nelson died at the Battle of Trafalger just before his ships claimed victory over the French; answers will vary

6. signers of the Declaration of Independence; answers will vary

7. Alfred Tennyson; 42 years from 1850-1892; *Idylls of the King*

8. Richard Saunders; answers will vary

9. leader in the Woman Suffrage Movement; Elizabeth Stanton and Matilda Gage

10. "Lady with the Lamp;" answers will vary

Who's Who In America
Study Guide

1. *Who's Who in America*

2. None; Marquis Who's Who, Inc.; Chicago, Ill.; 1982; 42nd

3. it provides information about the lives and careers of noteworthy individuals

4. answers will vary; however some of the Who's Who books are as follows: *Who Was Who in America, Who Was Who in American History* - Arts and Letters, *Who Was Who in American History* - The Military, *Who Was Who in American History* - Sciences and Technology, *Who's Who in the Midwest, Who's Who in the East, Who's Who in the South and Southwest, Who's Who in the West, Who's Who of American Women, Who's Who in Government, Who's Who in Finance and Industry, Who's Who in Religion, Who's Who in American Law,* and *Who's Who in the World*

5. they review, evaluate, and make general comments about information being published but do not select names appearing in *Who's Who in America*

6. names are arranged alphabetically by surnames; then names could be alphabetically arranged according to the first member of the compound

7. there is a table of abbreviations

8. There is a "Key to Information in this Directory" that gives you a sample of what information is provided and in what order; answers will vary, however, answers might include the following: name,

occupation, birthdate, parents' name, education, marital status, wife's name, children and their names, careers, religions, clubs, addresses, etc.

9. back of book in Volume II; a list of names of people whose biographical sketches appeared in the previous edition of *Who's Who in America* but have since retired; an index of names of people who appeared in the previous edition of *Who's Who in America* and are dead. Their biographical sketches with date of death and place of burial are published in the *Who Was Who in America*; back of book in Volume II, index on biographies found in Marquis *Who's Who Regional Directories*

Activity Sheet A

1. answers will vary
2. answers will vary
3. answers will vary
4. answers will vary
5. from biographees themselves, through questionnaires or through independent research by the Marquis staff; an asterisk is placed beside information gathered by Marquis staff

Activity Sheet B

1. the book gives, for each marriage, the spouse's name, the children born of that marriage, marriage date, and div if divorced; answers will vary
2. answers will vary
3. answers will vary
4. answers will vary; they tend to be members of organizations for areas of their specialization; answers will vary
5. the positon of responsibility held and the level of significant achievement attained in a career of noteworthy activity;
6. answers will vary

Almanac Study Guide

1. *The World Almanac*
2. Hann Umbarif Lane; Newspaper Enterprise Assoc., Inc.; N.Y.; 1984
3. from statistical publications, both governmental and private as well as from unpublished tabulations and records identified as "Unpublished data"
4. it is designed to serve as a convenient volume for statistical reference and as a guide to other statistical publications and sources
5. answers will vary
6. Each year tables and charts are reviewed and evaluated. New tables and charts are added, continuing series are brought up to date, and less timely data are curtailed or eliminated.
7. index or table of contents
8. consult source publications in libraries, write to agencies indicated in source notes to the tables, and write to the Bureau of the Census if source is cited

Activity Sheet A

1. Alaska; New York; Massachusetts
2. water, transportation; $34,075
3. 9.9 sec.; 1:15.18, 1:49.81
4. Oregon; answers will vary; potatoes and onions
5. $8.20; restrictions apply, consult post office, no parcel post service; greatest length 3½ feet, greatest length and girth combined, 6 feet

Activity Sheet B

1. 1899 - Friday; 1990 - Saturday; 2000 - Friday; 2015 - Tuesday

1817 - Thursday; 1893 - Monday; 1948 - Saturday; 2080 - Wednesday

2. 7-31 day time deposits, money market deposit accounts, 91-day certificates, super NOW accounts and others; answers will vary; answers will vary

3. 7-10 years old - 34 grams, or 11-14 years old - 45 grams; chicken, cottage cheese, lima beans

4. 9:00 AM; 11:00 AM; 6:00 AM; 17:00 (5:00 PM); 6:00 PM; standard time is determined from Greenwich, England the Prime Meridian of Longitude. The world is divided into 24 zones, each 15° of ark, or one hour in time. The zones to the east of the Prime Meridian are numbered minus 1-12, indicating the number of hours to be subtracted to obtain Greenwich Time. The zones to the west of the Prime Meridian are numbered plus 1-12 and hours must be added to get Greenwich Time.

5. Roger Hornsby

6. Marie, Michigan; 113 inches; Henry Ford, George Custer, Danny Thomas, Betty Hutton, Thomas Dewey, Will Kellog and others

7. Alaska, $16,257; $4638; no; answers will vary

8. answers will vary

9. Honolulu County, Hawaii; Phoenix, Arizona has a greater population — Phoenix / 789,704, and Honolulu / 762,874; answers will vary

Atlas
Study Guide

1. *Goode's World Atlas*

2. Edward B. Espenshade Jr.; Rand McNally and Co.; Chicago, Ill.; 1966

3. answers will vary, however answers may include maps that show political, physical, and climatic regions as well as natural vegetation, soil groups, density of population, major agriculture regions, locations of states, cities, and countries

4. distance, measured in degrees, north or south of the equator; distance, measured in degrees, east and west of a given meridian; degrees of latitude and longitudes are given on each map to help in locating city, country, state, etc.

5. an index that tells the degree of latitude and longitude with N,S,E,W as well as the page number where the map showing Lusaka is and the country or state where it is located

6. there is a legend that gives you the approximate distance of miles and/or kilometers per inch and/or centimeters

7. a relief legend that is color coded with number of meters and/or feet for each color

Activity Sheet A

1. Adriatic Sea; Split; Bari

2. answers will vary, however you may expect some of the following: Panama, Costa Rica, Kenya, Viet Nam, Cambodia, Sudan, Chad, and parts of many other countries along the equator.

3. answers will vary; answers will vary

4. Congo, The Congo, Angola, Caprivi Strip, Botswana; mostly mountains

5. Atlantic Ocean, Pacific Ocean, and Gulf of Mexico

6. answers will vary

7. answers will vary depending on year of publication

8. answers will vary

9. Yugoslavia; mixed-broadleaf deciduous and needleleaf evergreen trees; answers will vary

Activity Sheet B

1. Manihiki Island

2. answers will vary

3. answers will vary

4. approximately 10,200 miles; farther; approximately 3,700 farther from Brisbane, Australia to Rome, Italy than from Rome to New York City

5. Sweden; 57,725 square miles; Switzerland has more population per square miles than Sweden

6. Buenos Aires; 20-40 inches; humid subtropical

Reference Book **Review Sheet**

Note: Page numbers for references are not given because they will vary depending on edition used.

1. "I only regret that I have but one life to lose for my country." (*Familiar Quotations*)

2. 1633 (*Famous First Facts*)

3. answers will vary (*Current Biography Yearbook* or *Who's Who in America*)

4. Mrs. Maureen Weston; 449 hours (answers from 1984 edition) (*Guinness Book of World Records*)

5. answers will vary (*Familiar Quotations*)

6. answers will vary but may include: air traffic controller, mechanic, pilot, flight attendant, navigator (*Encyclopedia of Careers and Vocational Guidance*)

7. O'Henry; answers will vary (*Twentieth Century Authors*)

8. answers may vary but may include: strange, abnormal, bizarre, mishappen (*Thesaurus*)

9. Luxembourg borders Belgium, Germany, France (*Atlas*)

10. 1910; to Sheephead Bay, N.Y. (*Famous First Facts*)

11. *Sophie's Choice* (*Current Biography Yearbook*)

12. answers may vary but may include: Northeastern U.S., North-Central Europe, India, and the Far East (*Atlas* or *Almanac*)

13. answers may vary but may include learned, scholarly, literate, wise, authoritative (*Thesaurus*)

14. "Certainly there are lots of things in life that money won't buy, but it's very funny — Have you ever tried to buy them without money?" (*Familiar Quotations*)

15. Sandy Allen; 7 feet 7½ inches (*Guinness Book of World Records*)

16. an instrument for measuring blood pressure (*Dictionary*)

17. answers will vary but may include general education or a degree in business (*Encyclopedia of Careers and Vocational Guidance*)

18. −32°F; 113°F (*World Almanac*)

Chapter II

Readers' Guide To Periodical Literature **Study Guide**

1. *Reader's Guide to Periodical Literature*

2. H.G. Wilson and Co.; N.Y.; will vary depending on volume

3. a magazine

4. by author, subject and title

5. at the beginning of each volume is a key which explains all abbreviations

6. in the subject entry the subject is given first in bold type on a line by itself followed below by the article title and author. In the author entry the author's name appears in bold type on a line alone followed by the title of the article.

7. means that the articles under the heading suggested by "see also" might contain some information on the subject you've looked up

a "see" reference contains no articles but refers you to look under a different heading. A "see also" reference includes articles and suggests additional places to look for more information.

Activity Sheet A

1. answers will vary

2. answers will vary depending on volumed used

3.
   A. Je - June
   B. D - December
   C. bi-M - bimonthly - published two times a month
   D. pub - published
   E. jt. - Author - more than one author
   F. Ap - April
   G. q - quarterly - published four times a year
   H. cond - condensed - expressed in fewer words

4.
   A. Saturday Evening Post
   B. Scientific American
   C. Business Week
   D. New York Times Magazine

5. answers will vary
   A. answers will vary
   B. answers will vary

6. answers will vary

Review Sheet

1-5 answers will vary

Chapter III

Encyclopedia Study Guide

1. *World Book Encyclopedia*

2. Field Enterprises Educational Corporation; Merchandise Mart Plaza, Chicago, Ill.; 1983

3. an annual yearbook

4. yes; it helps you to locate the topics covered on a particular page

5. answers may vary; no; you can locate information by looking for topics alphabetically; a separate volume

6. answers may vary but may include maps, illustrations, diagrams, tables, charts, graphs

7. other topics that can be found in the encyclopedia that are related to the topic you are researching

8. general information in the *World Book Encyclopedia*. However, answers may vary depending on type of encyclopedia used

9.
   The Continent
   East Antarctica
   West Antarctica
   Climate
      The Antarctic Ocean
      Natural Resources
   Minerals
   Plant Life
   Land Animals
   Seals and Whales
   Birds
      Exploration
   Early Exploration
   Race for the South Pole
   American Exploration
   International Cooperation
   Antarctic Claims

Where In The World Am I?
Activity Sheet

1. *Tom Sawyer* - small Missouri town before Civil War; *War and Peace* - Russia, 1812, during Napolean's invasion of Russia; *A Tale of Two Cities* - London and Paris during the time of the French Revolution; answers will vary

2. answers will vary but should include: Jesse James and Billy the Kid - symbolized outlaws of that era; Wyatt Earp and Wild Bill Hickok - gained fame as fearless defenders of law and order; answers will vary

3. all are deserts; answers will vary but should include: area covered with sand and gravel, soil too hot to support much vegetation, oil and natural gas under many areas; answers will vary

4. answers will vary but should include: Little Big Horn - scene of battle between Custer and his troops and the Indians on the Montana Territory by Little Big Horn River, much controversy surrounds Custer's attack; Yorktown - Virginia, scene of Cornwallis' surrender to the Colonial Army which ended the Revolutionary War; Hiroshima - Japan, where first atomic bomb was dropped on Aug. 6, 1945. Bomb destroyed 4.7 square miles and over 92,000 people were reported killed or missing; answers will vary

5. largest city in Morocco, North Africa; answers will vary

Piñatas, Fireworks, And Totem Poles
Activity Sheet

1. animals, people, and pictures to represent other clan emblems; help and protect the tribe, as part of their religious ceremonies; answers will vary

2. pyrotechnics; Independence Day (4th of July); as danger signals, as signals of help, to light up landing strips and battlefields; answers will vary

3. answers will vary but may include: London Bridge, hopscotch, leapfrog, hide and seek, blindman's bluff, jump rope; answers will vary

4. the ring: from the ancient custom of using a ring to seal any type of important agreement
   the veil: from the Roman custom of having the bride wear a full-length veil that was later used as a burial shroud
   carrying the bride over the threshold: from the ancient practice of capturing a wife

5. on cave paintings; birth of children, marriage, death, to gain courage for battle, drive away evil spirits, celebrate victory, make rain
   Japan: ancient court dance
   China: drive away evil spirits
   India: tells legends of Hindu gods and heroes
   New Mexico: performed at religious ceremonies
   Greeks: warriors practiced movements of attack and defense

6. to explain natural phenomena; most had human qualities and resembled humans although they had supernatural powers; legends may have been created for amusement while myths are considered sacred and true; many ancients thought the serpent was a symbol of health and they pictured the god of health holding a staff with a serpent coiled around it; Cupid, the Roman god of love shot arrows into victims causing them to fall in love.

What Makes It Tick?
Activity Sheet

1. answers will vary; answers will vary; answers will vary; to protect yourself from anyone copying your idea without paying; Samuel Hopkins; a new way of getting lye for soap from wood ashes

2. Magnesia, the name of a region in ancient Greece; a Greek shepherd boy rested his iron-tipped shepherd's crook against a rock. When he tried to move it, the rock held it tight; magnetic or loderstone; answers will vary

3. a periscope; a periscope has prisms to reflect the light and lenses to make ships that are far away show clearly; answers will vary

4. phosphorus; glass, glue, and a chemical that gives off oxygen; paraffin; so it will light easily; John Walker; 1827; a splint

of wood with the end coated with melted sulfur. The splints were used for carrying fire from place to place. They could not be lit by striking them; a splint of wood had a head made of a mixture of chemicals. The head was lighted by holding it in a bottle filled with asbestos soaked in strong acid.

5. Hans Lippershay; an eye glass maker; 1608; a boy who was working for Lippershay a spectaclemaker happened to hold one lens in front of another and looked through them. He found this made things he was looking at seem much closer. Lippershay put the two lenses in a tube and called it a telescope; Galileo; he is a famous scientist often called the Father of Science. He discovered the idea of the pendulum which paved the way for the first good clocks. He was the first person to see mountains on the moon and sunspots on the sun. He discovered that Jupiter has moons traveling around it and many other things about the planets and stars.

6. a refracting telescope is made with lens while a reflecting telescope is made with mirrors; Yerkes Observatory, Williams Bay, Wisconsin; 40 inches across; Hale telescope, Mt. Palomar, California

Somewhere Over the Rainbow Activity Sheet

1. Bermuda Triangle; the area included within the traingle formed from Melbourne, Florida, to Bermuda, to Puerto Rico; planes and ships have disappeared without a trace; answers will vary; answers will vary

2. solar eclipse: the sun appears darkened as the moon passes between the sun and the earth
lunar eclipse: moon appears darkened as it moves into earth's shadow
solar eclipse; viewing one directly can damage vision

3. a group of stars within a definite region of the sky; answers will vary

4. begins where atmosphere is too thin to affect objects moving through it — usually 100 miles above earth; gravity; acceleration effects, oxygen, extreme temperatures, radiation, weightlessness, etc.

5. answers will vary

6. answers will vary

7. July 20, 1969; Neil Armstrong; "That's one small step for a man, one giant leap for mankind."; answers will vary

All Animals Great and Small Activity Sheet

1. because animals were not crossbred as they are today; because humans developed different breeds to serve many purposes and as a result today there are many types of dogs; answers will vary; answers will vary

2. answers will vary; answers will vary, however you may expect the following: because of the climate, food sources, and the animals were never brought to a particular continent and they didn't migrate

3. answers will vary, however the bandicoot, wombat, kangaroo, koala, flying phalangers are examples of pouched animals; Australia; opossum; answers may vary, however, most answers will state that animals live in the pouch because they are tiny and underdeveloped when they are born; marsupial

4. the dog; answers may vary; answers will vary

5. orangutan, chimpanzee, gorilla, gibbon; gorilla; chimpanzee; orangutan; gibbon; apes have no tails

6. earth pig; double life; white; to creep; soft nose horn; answers will vary

Encyclopedia
Review Sheet

1. by the volcano of Mount Vesuvius in A.D. 79

2. answers will vary

3. Wisconsin, Illinois, Kentucky, Tennessee, Mississippi, Iowa, Missouri, Arkansas, Louisiana, Minnesota; Old Man River

4. God of War; Mars

5. answers will vary but may include pit vipers (i.e. rattlesnake, water moccasin, copperhead, and coral snakes)

6. answers will vary

7. volume "H" Holiday; volume "S" Saint Valentine

8. answers will vary

Chapter IV

Bibliography
Activity Sheet

1. answers will vary

2. at the end of the chapter or collected at the end of book

3. and others; pages; volume; editor, edited by, or edition

4. Alcott, Louisa Mae. Little Women. New York: Scholastic Book Services, 1960. The World Book Encyclopedia, 1962 ed. S.v. "Painting."

5. answers will vary

6. answers will vary

7. answers will vary

8. author or editor, name of book and title of article, place of publication, publisher, date of publication,

9. answers will vary

Footnotes/Endnotes

1. answers will vary but may include that it authenticates the information

2. answers will vary but may include that it helps the reader to know the source of information

3. "in the same place;" means that the source is the same as the preceding cited source

4. at end of chapter, at bottom of page, or collected at the end of book

5. Robert Louis Stevenson, Kidnapped (New York: Lancer Books, Inc., 1967), p.4. Issac Asimov, "The Next Frontier?" National Geographic, July 1976, pp. 76-89.

6. answers will vary but may include direct quotes and statistics

7. answers will vary

8. answers will vary

Chapter V

Focusing Topics

1. answers will vary
2. answers will vary
3. answers will vary

Selecting Reference Books

1. answers will vary; answers will vary
2. answers will vary; answers will vary
3. answers will vary; answers will vary
4. answers will vary; answers will vary

Organizing And Outlining Research Topics

outlines will vary; research papers will vary